Giants in the Landscape: Monumentality and Territories in the European Neolithic

Proceedings of the XVII UISPP World Congress (1–7 September, Burgos, Spain)

Volume 3 / Session A25d

Edited by

Vincent Ard and Lucile Pillot

Archaeopress Archaeology

ARCHAEOPRESS PUBLISHING LTD
Gordon House
276 Banbury Road
Oxford OX2 7ED

www.archaeopress.com

ISBN 978 1 78491 285 7
ISBN 978 1 78491 286 4 (e-Pdf)

© Archaeopress, UISPP and authors 2016

VOLUME EDITORS: Vincent Ard and Lucile Pillot

SERIES EDITOR: The board of UISPP

SERIES PROPERTY: UISPP – International Union of Prehistoric and Protohistoric Sciences

The editing of this volume was funded by the Instituto Terra e Memória, Centro de Geociências UID/Multi/00073/2013, with the support of the Fundação para a Ciência e Tecnologia FCT/MEC)

KEY-WORDS IN THIS VOLUME: Neolithic – Landscape – Territory – Organization

UISPP PROCEEDINGS SERIES is a print on demand and an open access publication, edited by UISPP through Archaeopress

BOARD OF UISPP: Jean Bourgeois (President), Luiz Oosterbeek (Secretary-General), François Djindjian (Treasurer), Ya-Mei Hou (Vice President), Marta Arzarello (Deputy Secretary-General). The Executive Committee of UISPP also includes the Presidents of all the international scientific commissions (www.uispp.org)

BOARD OF THE XVII WORLD CONGRESS OF UISPP: Eudald Carbonell (Secretary-General), Robert Sala I Ramos, Jose Maria Rodriguez Ponga (Deputy Secretary-Generals)

All rights reserved. No part of this book may be reproduced, or transmitted, in any form or by any means, electronic, mechanical, photocopying or otherwise, without the prior written permission of the copyright owners.

This book is available direct from Archaeopress or from our website www.archaeopress.com

Contents

List of Figures and Tables ii

Foreword to the XVII UISPP Congress Proceedings Series Edition iv

Introduction v

Acknowledgments vi

Chapter 1 – Northern and Eastern Europe: UK and Poland

Megalithic tombs, barrows, and enclosures in fourth millennium BC Britain 3
Timothy DARVILL

House and megalith. Some remarks on the Niedźwiedź type tombs in the Eastern group
    of the TRB culture 19
Seweryn RZEPECKI

Chapter 2 – Western Europe: France

The role of enclosures in territorial organization in the Paris Basin between
    4500 and 3800 BC 31
Claira LIETAR

Late Neolithic graves and enclosures in Lower Languedoc: A phenomenon of alternation,
    3200-2200 cal. BC 45
Luc JALLOT

Chapter 3 – Southern Europe: Spain and Portugal

Prehistoric ditched enclosures and necropolises in Southern Iberia:
    a diachronic overview 57
Víctor JIMÉNEZ-JÁIMEZ AND José Enrique MÁRQUEZ-ROMERO

Ditched enclosures and the ideologies of death in the Late Neolithic and
    Chalcolithic South Portugal 69
António Carlos VALERA

Towards a definition of the prehistoric landscape in the Plateau of *Sigarra*:
    visibility and territoriality between the Middle Neolithic and Bronze Age 85
Natalia SALAZAR ORTIZ

List of Figures and Tables

Chapter 1 – Northern and Eastern Europe: UK and Poland

T. DARVILL: Megalithic tombs, barrows, and enclosures in fourth millennium BC Britain

Figure 1a. Distribution of Neolithic monuments for the period 3800-3300 BC. Long barrows 6
Figure 1b. Distribution of Neolithic monuments for the period 3800-3300 BC. Causewayed enclosures. 7
Figure 2. Location of the enclosures and long barrows on Hambledon Hill, Dorset 9
Figure 3. Location of Crickley Hill and the Peak Camp on the Cotswold escarpment 10
Figure 4. Idealized settlement pattern in areas with long barrows and enclosures 14

S. RZEPECKI: House and megalith. Some remarks on the Niedźwiedź type tombs in the Eastern group of the TRB culture

Figure 1. Distribution of the Niedźwiedź type tombs in Poland 20
Figure 2. Sarnowo and Niedźwiedź type tombs 21
Figure 3. Niedźwiedź type tombs 23
Figure 4. Danubian houses and Niedźwiedź type tombs 25

Chapter 2 – Western Europe: France

C. LIETAR: The role of enclosures in territorial organization in the Paris Basin between 4500 and 3800 BC

Figure 1. Enclosures classified by hierarchical ranks for the Middle Neolithic II (4250-3950 BC) 33
Figure 2. Modelling of environmental contexts for the Aisne-Vesle sector 35
Figure 3. Size of the enclosures: ratio of the overall perimeter ditches 38
Figure 4. Scales of procurement of tertiary flint from the plain of Cuiry-lès-Chaudardes 40

L. JALLOT: Late Neolithic graves and enclosures in Lower Languedoc: A phenomenon of alternation, 3200-2200 cal. BC

Figure 1. A: styles of habitats in the Fontbouisse culture (2600-2200 cal. BC) 48
Figure 2. A: the enclosure of Boussargues 50

Chapter 3 – Southern Europe: Spain and Portugal

V. JIMÉNEZ-JÁIMEZ AND J. E. MÁRQUEZ-ROMERO: Prehistoric ditched enclosures and necropolises in Southern Iberia: a diachronic overview

Figure 1. Maps showing the geographical distribution of Neolithic and Copper Age 58
Figure 2. Perdigões and its spatial relations with Neolithic megalithic tombs (antas) 61
Figure 3. Floor plan of La Pijotilla (Badajoz) ditched enclosure 64

A. C. VALERA: Ditched enclosures and the ideologies of death in the Late Neolithic and Chalcolithic South Portugal

Figure 1. Distribution of enclosures in Portugal 71
Figure 2. Radiocarbon dates available for South Portugal ditched enclosures 73
Figure 3. Gate orientations 74
Figure 4. Landscape of Perdigões enclosure 75
Figure 5. Outeiro Alto 2 76
Figure 6. A- Perdigões eastern necropolis; B- Porto Torrão peripheral necropolis 78
Figure 7. Porto Torrão ditch with depositions of human remains 79
Figure 8. Bela Vista 5 enclosure, with central pit burial of a woman. 80
Table 1. Radiocarbon dates available for South Portugal ditched enclosures 72

N. SALAZAR ORTIZ: Towards a definition of the prehistoric landscape in the Plateau of Sigarra: visibility and territoriality between the Middle Neolithic and Bronze Age

Figure 1. Location of the plateau of Sigarra on the Iberian Peninsula map 86
Figure 2. List of sites and their chronologies used in calculating Neolithic visibility patterns 89

FIGURE 3. MAP OF THE NEOLITHIC VISIBILITY PATTERNS (5500-2200 CAL. BC)..90
FIGURE 4. THE MEGALITH OF LA PERA (PINÓS)..91
FIGURE 5. LIST OF SITES AND THEIR CHRONOLOGIES USED IN CALCULATING CHALCOLITHIC-BRONZE AGE...................92
FIGURE 6. MAP OF THE CHALCOLITHIC-BRONZE AGE VISIBILITY PATTERNS (2200-700 CAL. BC)................................93

Foreword to the XVII UISPP Congress Proceedings Series Edition

Luiz OOSTERBEEK
Secretary-General

UISPP has a long history, starting with the old International Association of Anthropology and Archaeology, back in 1865, until the foundation of UISPP itself in Bern, in 1931, and its growing relevance after WWII, from the 1950's. We also became members of the International Council of Philosophy and Human Sciences, associate of UNESCO, in 1955.

In its XIVth world congress in 2001, in Liège, UISPP started a reorganization process that was deepened in the congresses of Lisbon (2006) and Florianópolis (2011), leading to its current structure, solidly anchored in more than twenty-five international scientific commissions, each coordinating a major cluster of research within six major chapters: Historiography, methods and theories; Culture, economy and environments; Archaeology of specific environments; Art and culture; Technology and economy; Archaeology and societies.

The XVIIth world congress of 2014, in Burgos, with the strong support of Fundación Atapuerca and other institutions, involved over 1700 papers from almost 60 countries of all continents. The proceedings, edited in this series but also as special issues of specialized scientific journals, will remain as the most important outcome of the congress.

Research faces growing threats all over the planet, due to lack of funding, repressive behavior and other constraints. UISPP moves ahead in this context with a strictly scientific programme, focused on the origins and evolution of humans, without conceding any room to short term agendas that are not root in the interest of knowledge.

In the long run, which is the terrain of knowledge and science, not much will remain from the contextual political constraints, as severe or dramatic as they may be, but the new advances into understanding the human past and its cultural diversity will last, this being a relevant contribution for contemporary and future societies.

This is what UISPP is for, and this is also why we are currently engaged in contributing for the relaunching of Human Sciences in their relations with social and natural sciences, namely collaborating with the International Year of Global Understanding, in 2016, and with the World Conference of the Humanities, in 2017.

The next two congresses of UISPP, in Melbourn (2017) and in Geneva (2020), will confirm this route.

Introduction

Vincent Ard and Lucile Pillot

In many European areas, the Neolithic period corresponds to the development of architectural monumentality which left important marks in the landscape, as well as the land clearing and the cultivation by the first agro-pastoral societies. This monumentality can be observed in the domestic sphere, particularly by the edification of enclosures with various functions and surfaces, and in the funeral and ritual sphere, by the development of many megalithic or non megalithic tombs.

It's noteworthy that the concomitant or non concomitant development of these monumental sites reveals the complexity of cultural, symbolic and socio-economic practices of Neolithic societies.

These monumental sites probably reflect socio-cultural dynamic systems in which the notion of territory seems to be a fundamental concept. Obviously, in many areas of Europe, Neolithic people have appropriated their surrounding landscape, exploited or not, by the edification of these monumental sites. In this way, they probably sustain their control over a definite territory. That's why burial, domestic or even defensive monumental sites, must be jointly analyzed in order to understand the organization of these Neolithic spaces.

Part of the XVII World UISPP Congress, held in Burgos (Spain), the 4th September 2014, our session untitled '*Monumentality and territory: relationship between enclosures and necropolis in the European Neolithic*' examined different questions:
1. The various manifestations of the relationship between Neolithic enclosures and tombs in different contexts of Europe, notably through spatial analysis.
2. The concept of landscape appropriation, combining domestic, symbolic, economic or natural spaces.
3. The patterns of territorial organization, in which enclosures and tombs have a fundamental role in some Neolithic contexts.

The present proceedings give an overview of these questions with eight case studies coming from different parts of Europe. For the Northern and Eastern Europe, T. Darvill and S. Rzepecki give insights about the development of architectural monumentality and the close links between enclosures and tombs in Britain and Poland.

Then, two French case studies (C. Lietar and L. Jallot) show the state of research in Western Europe where the development of monumental sites is non synchronic and participate to the appropriation of landscape and the construction of territories.

Finally, examples from Southern Europe (Spain and Portugal), give by V Jiménez-Jáimez and J. E. Márquez-Romero, A. C. Valera and N. Salazar Ortiz, explain the complexity of the symbolic and spatial relation between enclosures and the world of the death.

Acknowledgments

We would like to thank the local organizers of the UISPP Congress, particularly Luiz Oosterbeek who follow the preparation of these proceedings, and Archaeopress for the edition of this book. We are also grateful to Rui Boaventura, Karim Gernigon and Juan F. Gibaja Bao for the reviewing of some of these papers.

Chapter 1

Northern and Eastern Europe: UK and Poland

Megalithic tombs, barrows, and enclosures in fourth millennium BC Britain

Timothy DARVILL

Department of Archaeology, Anthropology and Forensic Science, Faculty of Science and Technology, Bournemouth University, Dorset BH12 5BB. United Kingdom
tdarvill@bournemouth.ac.uk

Abstract

The date and distribution across Britain of megalithic monuments and related structures dating to the fourth millennium BC is briefly outlined, together with on overview of contemporary enclosures. Studies of the distribution of human body parts show that in southern Britain during the period c. 3800-3300 BC long barrows and oval barrows were built and used by the same communities that also created causewayed enclosures. The situation in western and northern Britain is less clear as few enclosures are known and preservation conditions militate against the survival of human remains. A simple model involving local and regional articulations between enclosures and burial monuments is briefly outlined.

Keywords: *causewayed enclosures, megalithic tombs, long barrows, oval barrows, settlement patterns*

Résumé

La datation et la répartition des monuments mégalithiques et des structures associées datées du 4ᵉ millénaire avant notre ère sont brièvement décrits, tout comme un état des lieux des connaissances sur les enceintes contemporaines. L'étude de la distribution des os humains par partie anatomique montre que dans le sud de la Grande-Bretagne, des longs tumulus et des tumulus ovales sont construits entre 3800 et 3300 av. J.-C. et utilisés par les mêmes communautés qui ont creusé les enceintes à fossés interrompus. La situation dans l'ouest et le nord de la Grande-Bretagne est moins évidente car peu d'enceintes sont connues et des problèmes taphonomiques ne permettent pas la conservation des restes humains. Enfin, un modèle territorial simple illustrant les relations entre enceintes et sites funéraires aux échelles locale et régionale est brièvement présenté.

Most-clés: *enceintes à fossés interrompus, tombes mégalithiques, longs tumulus, tumulus ovalaires, trames territoriales*

Introduction

Megalithic monuments have been recognized and studied in many parts of Britain since the seventeenth century AD when antiquarian scholars and travellers first marvelled at the rude stone structures and great mounds (Michell 1982). Since that time our understanding of the date and variety of such monuments has expanded considerably. It is now clear that various styles were preferred by communities living in different parts of Britain during the course of the fourth and third millennia BC, and that in areas where stone was scarce or absent such structures were often made of earth and wood (Ashbee 1984). By contrast, enclosures of the kind that can now be assigned to the fourth and third millennia BC were not recognized as a distinct class of archaeological monument until the early twentieth century AD when research in Wiltshire and Sussex (Curwen 1930) showed that earthworks characterized by interrupted ditches dated to the Neolithic period (Piggott 1954: 18-32). In this paper attention is first directed towards current interpretations of the core evidence for megalithic monuments, barrows, and enclosures across the island of Britain (England, Scotland and Wales) before turning to the question of the relationships between such monuments.

Megalithic tombs and related monuments

There is a very wide range of megalithic and non-megalithic burial monuments dated to the fourth and third millennia BC across Britain, many with similarities to structures found on the near continent in France, Netherlands, northern Germany, and southern Scandinavia, as well as in Ireland. Although detailed inventories exist for Scotland (Henshall 1963, 1972; Henshall and Ritchie 1995, 2001; Davidson and Henshall 1989, 1991), the situation for England, Wales, and the major islands around their coasts is less good. The overview by Daniel (1950) remains useful, and can be complemented by a series of national studies (Ashbee 1984; Kinnes 1979; 1992) and regional reviews (for example Powell *et al.* 1969; Lynch 1976; Smith *et al.* 1979; Philp and Dutto 1985; Barker 1992; Darvill 2004). The following summary is based on a recent overview of the evidence in its wider context (Darvill 2010: 103-117).

Multi-period monuments are common (Corcoran 1972) and provide stratigraphic evidence for the succession of structures at a particular site. Taken together such sequences help inform understandings of the constantly changing distribution of preferred architectural styles. As a general rule, monuments gradually mutate from simple closed inaccessible chambers and burial zones with relatively few interments through to large, open, and easily accessible chambers containing the remains of many individuals (Bradley 1998: 60). But there are many exceptions to the rule and many local traditions. Likewise, the shape of covering mounds varies greatly: round, oval, square, rectangular, and trapezoidal are all common. Some monuments, such as dolmens, portal dolmens, and timber mortuary houses, were not normally encapsulated within a mound at all but may have been surrounded by a low platform. In some cases these simple essentially open structures later became incorporated into larger, mounded, monuments.

In the west of Britain some of the simplest monuments, known as 'dolmens', were made by raising a large block of stone above the ground, supported by stumpy-looking orthostats. At some, such as Cerreg Samson, Pembrokeshire, there is evidence that the raised stone was an earthfast boulder that had been elevated over the spot where it originally lay (Lynch 1975). A more elaborate style of dolmen is the so-called 'portal dolmen' or 'portal tomb' whose distribution includes southwestern England, the north Cotswolds, Wales, and most of Ireland where by far the greatest concentration is known. Characteristically, portal dolmens comprise four or more large upright slabs supporting a single capstone with the front of the tomb defined by three of the uprights set in an H-shaped formation (Kytmannow 2008).

Across eastern and southern Britain, where large stones for building were scarce, simple timber mortuary houses are well represented, usually as tent-like structures or timber boxes (Ashbee 1969). Most were constructed by splitting a large tree-trunk, generally oak, down the middle to provide a pair of D-shaped posts for either end the chamber. Once the two posts were securely set in the ground a chamber was formed in the gap between using smaller timbers and panels of wattle-work. Structures that are very similar to those in Britain are well-known amongst the northern TRB monuments of Jutland, especially mortuary houses defined as the Konens Høj Type (Madsen 1979).

Across much of Scotland, the northeastern England, and a handful of areas further south, round barrows were the most common form of fourth millennium BC burial monument (Leary *et al.* 2010). Most simply comprise mounds of earth and stone, sometimes carefully layered, covering a central burial pit, cremation trench, closed stone chamber, or some kind of above-ground wooden chamber. Some were surrounded by quarry ditches, which often survive as ring-ditches even where the mound has gone. A detailed study of these monuments Ian Kinnes catalogued more than 80 examples but he suggested that as many as 20,000 might once have existed (Kinnes 1979). A variant of the round barrow involves covering the burial pit or chamber with an elongated oval-shaped mound. Presumably the difference is one born of projecting a particular identity onto the world because the basic arrangements inside are otherwise identical between the two traditions. Less widespread than round barrows, oval barrows are mainly confined to southeastern Britain. At Wayland's Smithy, Oxfordshire, an oval barrow 14 m by 7 m was built over the decayed remains of the timber mortuary house in 3520-3470 BC, less than a century after its initial construction (Whittle 1991; Bayliss and Whittle 2007: 117-119).

Along the western coastlands and extending inland to a few areas such as the north Cotswolds and the Peak District of Derbyshire are a light scatter of simple passage graves of continental type that also occur in Ireland at the same time. They are characterized by a round or slightly oval mound covering a centrally placed stone-built chamber that was connected to the outside of the mound by a straight passage thereby allowing continued access to the burial area. At Broadsands, Torbay, an example excavated in 1958 contained four small groups of human remains associated with Carinated Bowl pottery and worked flints dated to the period 3900-3700 BC (Sheridan *et al.* 2008). Typologically, the monument finds strong paralleled with sites such as Guennoc II (Finistère), France, dating to about 4000 BC and Pavia Type monuments in Portugal that are still older. In north Wales, Anglesey, the western Isles, and Orkney much larger so-called developed passage graves appear after about 3300 BC, part of a tradition whose heartland lies in the Boyne Valley of eastern Ireland (Herity 1974).

Soon after 3800 BC a new kind of monument became fashionable across Britain, and remained so for two or three centuries. These were long barrows, and they are characterized by a large rectangular or trapezoidal mound usually covering one or more burial chambers. At one end of the mound there is usually a substantial façade of some kind, sometimes with a forecourt in front to form an arena for ceremonies. In some cases the chambers open directly from the façade or the back of the forecourt (known as terminal chambers) while in others the chambers open from the long sides of the mound (lateral chambers). Long barrows are often orientated roughly east-west, but it is clear that pre-existing monuments on the site sometimes over-ride this rule. Local topography was also important in the positioning of sites and many are set near the top of steep slopes with broad views in some directions, very limited views in others, and almost always overlooking a spring or the headwaters of a major river-system. Broadly similar monuments are also known in Ireland and throughout the Atlantic coastlands of Europe from the Loire to the Baltic, as well as some inland areas on the Continent. Large specimens, like West Kennet, Wiltshire, or Na Tri Shean, Highland, measure 100 m or more long, and while smaller examples are common, all represent a considerable amount of energy expended on their construction. In some places long barrows were added to whatever stood on the site already, covering it completely with wholly new chambers or sometimes extending and remodelling existed structures. Elsewhere, long barrows appear to have been planned as a unitary structure, coherent in design and constructed as a single operation. In all cases, however, it is notable that the chambers rarely occupy more than about five per cent of the total area of the monument (cf. Fleming 1972; 1973).

Several thousand long barrows are extant across the country, especially where they have not been disturbed by later activity (Figure 1A). Their widespread distribution reflects the expansion of farming settlement between 3800 BC and 3500 BC. Nevertheless, broad regional groupings can be discerned on the basis of common styles in tomb design. Thus for example a Cotswold-Severn Group, North Wales Group, Clyde Group, Northeastern Group, Midlands Group, Wessex Group, and a Medway Group can be recognized. The fashion for long barrows was fairly short-lived. Few were built after 3500 BC, and those still in use were often deliberately blocked up or subject to some final ritual event. Curiously, many of the other types of monument mentioned above – for example various kinds of dolmen, round barrows, oval barrows, and passage – continue to be constructed and used through the later fourth millennium BC and in many cases through into the third millennium BC.

Enclosures

Across much of southern Britain large ditched or walled enclosures were built in the centuries after 3700 BC (Darvill and Thomas 2001; Oswald *et al.* 2001; Whittle *et al.* 2011; and see Darvill 2010: 96-103 for a summary of the evidence). Variously called camps, causewayed camps, causewayed enclosures, enclosures, or interrupted ditch systems the terminology reflects the apparent diversity of field evidence while recognizing that the ditches defining many (but not all) were dug as a series of elongated pits separated by narrow causeways. Spoil from the ditches was used to build a rampart or wall inside the ditch, usually continuous except for the main entranceways. Largely thanks to aerial

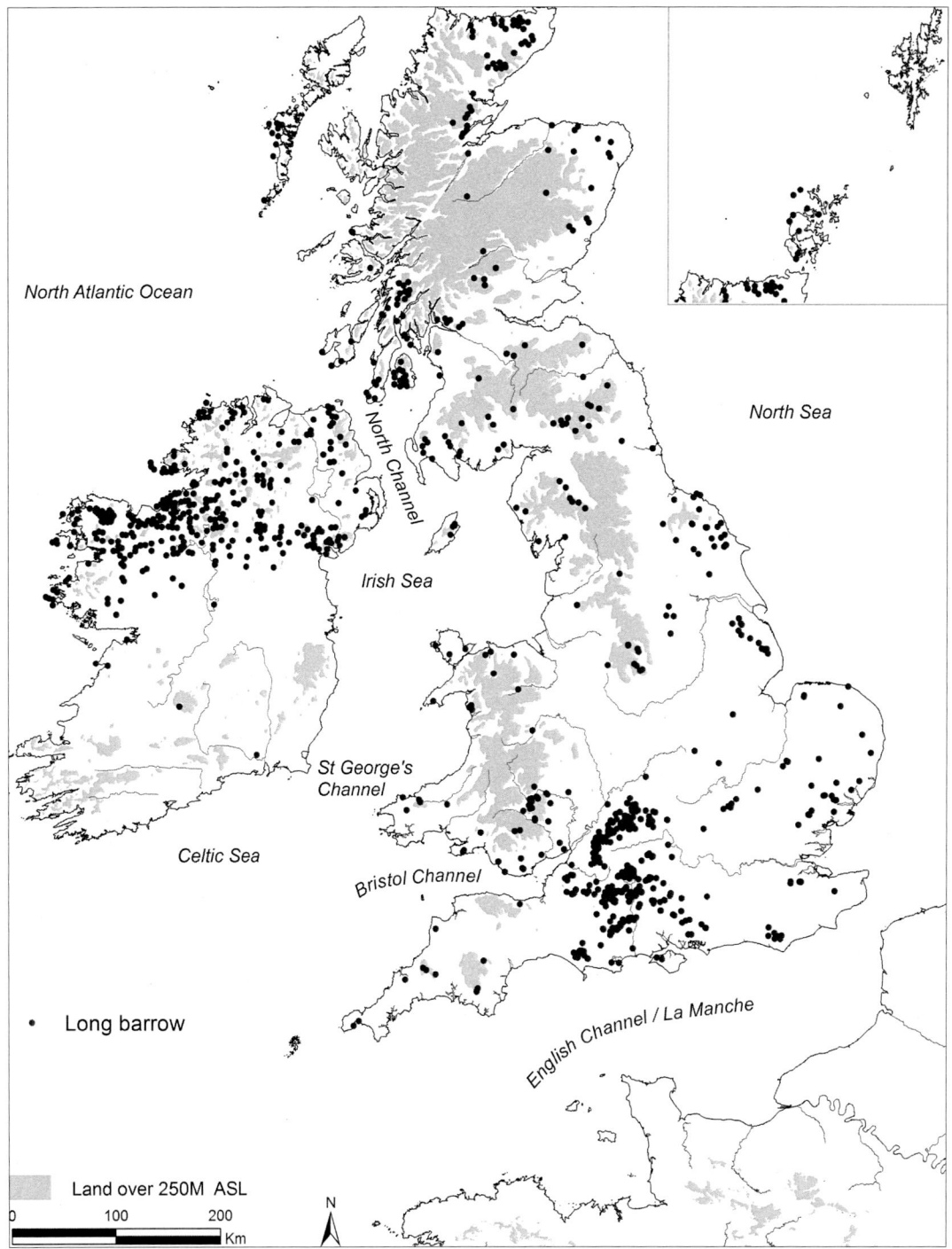

FIGURE 1A. DISTRIBUTION OF NEOLITHIC MONUMENTS FOR THE PERIOD 3800-3300 BC. LONG BARROWS. (FROM DARVILL 2010: FIGURE 39).

photography the number of these sites known has doubled since 1970 so that over 100 examples can now be cited (Palmer 1976; Oswald *et al.* 2001). Not all have been confirmed by excavation and so far there are no convincing examples in northern England or Scotland (Figure 1B). In southern Britain they occur in a variety of positions including hilltop and promontory situations, hillslopes, and valley floors. Many appear to have been built in light woodland or small clearances. Their size, construction, and the scale of the boundary ditches, vary greatly. On a wider, continental scale, the British examples appear relatively late in the overall sequence, but contemporary with other regional

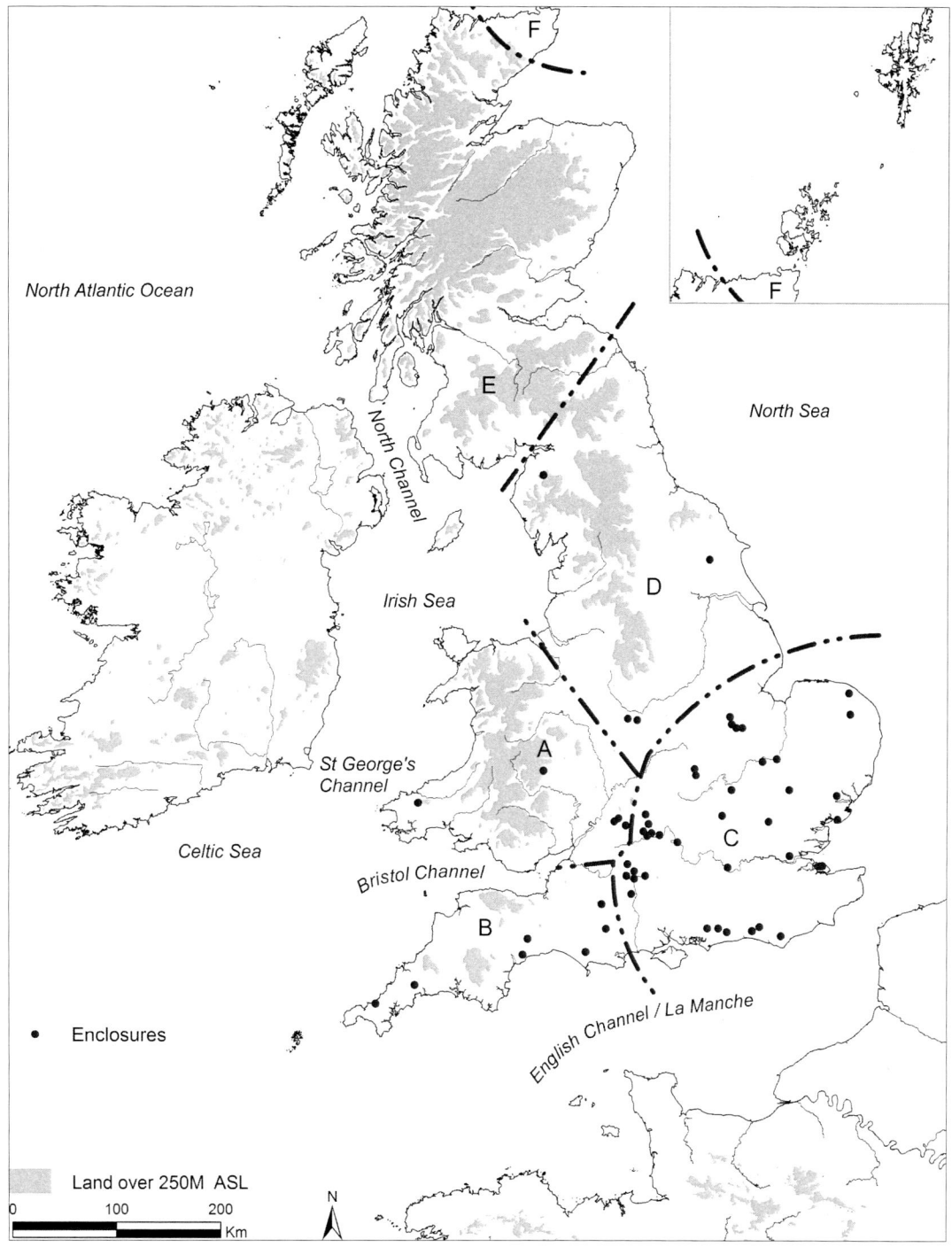

FIGURE 1B. DISTRIBUTION OF NEOLITHIC MONUMENTS FOR THE PERIOD 3800-3300 BC.
CAUSEWAYED ENCLOSURES. (FROM DARVILL 2010: FIGURE 33).

expressions of the enclosure tradition in western France, the late Michelsberg Cultures of eastern France and the Rhineland, and the TRB Cultures of north Germany / southern Scandinavia (Klassen 2014: 211-219).

Much debate has surrounded the interpretation of these enclosures and they have variously been seen as settlements, cattle enclosures, ceremonial centres, excarnation sites, trade and exchange centres, and periodic festival sites (Oswald *et al.* 2001: 123-131). But simplicity of purpose and modern distinctions between settlements and ceremonial places are not especially helpful, and many enclosures can best be interpreted as settlements, either temporary or permanent, which also acted as meeting places and provide an arena for ceremonies and rituals. The interior of most enclosures contain a variety of features including houses, pits, and, on occasions, burials. Sometimes there is such a profusion of features that interpretation is difficult, while elsewhere severe erosion prevents full appraisal of the arrangements inside. Ditches usually prove rich in artefacts. Some material suggests localized deliberate structured deposition, but broken pottery, animal bones, flintwork, axes and tools, and worn-out querns is sufficiently widespread to suggest that the ditches were frequently used as middens. Soil was occasionally thrown over these deposits, probably to stifle the smell inevitably associated with such dumps. This practice, coupled with the problems caused by the occasional collapse of the internal ramparts necessitated periodic re-digging of the ditches. Such re-digging the ditches has been used as evidence to support the idea that enclosures were subject to periodic occupation, perhaps for festivals of some kind when the population from scattered farmsteads gathered together at a central point. The fairly regular spacing of enclosures on the chalklands in Sussex and Wiltshire adds further weight to this idea and it is tempting to suggest that such activities were responsible for the origins of many enclosures.

Like long barrows, causewayed enclosures seem to have a fairly limited lifespan and few were built after 3300 BC (Whittle *et al.* 2011: 705). The final hours of occupation at Crickley Hill, Gloucestershire, in around 3450 BC witnessed a victorious attack on the settlement, which was then sacked and burnt. Hundreds of flint leaf-shaped arrowheads littering the ramparts and gateways were found during excavations through the 1970s and early 80s (Dixon 1988). After 3300 BC rather different kinds of enclosure start to appear and continue into the third millennium BC. These include henge enclosures, classic henges, C-shaped enclosures, and a range of palisaded enclosures (Harding and Lee 1987; Gibson 2002).

Linking barrows and enclosures

For a few centuries in the middle part of the fourth millennium BC, from about 3700 to 3300 BC, long barrows and causewayed enclosures seem to have been contemporary components of the settlement patterns found in the landscapes of southern Britain. A possible connection between them was first recognized in the early 1960s by Isobel Smith while writing up the earlier excavations carried out by Alexander Keiller at Windmill Hill, Wiltshire. She identified the possibility that activities within and around the enclosure could be related to the use of the West Kennet Long Barrow 3 km away to the south (Piggott 1962: 68; Smith 1965). The main evidence prompting this idea was the differential presence of human remains at the two sites: skulls and long bones in the ditch fills of the causewayed enclosure and the relative absence of these same skeletal elements within the chambers of the long barrow. Initially it was just a casual observation, but later work by Nick Thorpe (1984) gave qualitative and quantitative precision to the picture which he extended to an analysis of other assemblages from enclosures and barrow sites. However, crucial to the integrity of the argument was the contemporaneity of paired sites. Similarities in the pottery assemblages suggested that they were close, but it was not until detailed dating sequences became available that the two came into exact coincidence. The West Kennet long barrow contains the remains of around 46 individuals including men, women and children deposited over a relatively short period. The excavated primary deposits date to the period 3670-3635 BC and the last interments to 3640-3610 BC (Bayliss and Whittle 2007). Detailed dating of the construction sequence at Windmill Hill shows that inner ditch was constructed around 3685-3635 BC, the outer ditch at around the same time, 3685-3610 BC, and the middle ditch just slightly later at 3655-3605 BC (Whittle *et al.* 2011: 81-93). Chronologically, the structural sequence at Windmill Hill maps very well indeed with the burial sequence at West Kennet and it is therefore very probable that those buried in West Kennet participated in the construction and use of Windmill Hill.

Elsewhere in central southern England similar patterns can be seen. Almost all known causewayed enclosures have a long barrow within 5 km, often closer. Whether the reverse is also true cannot

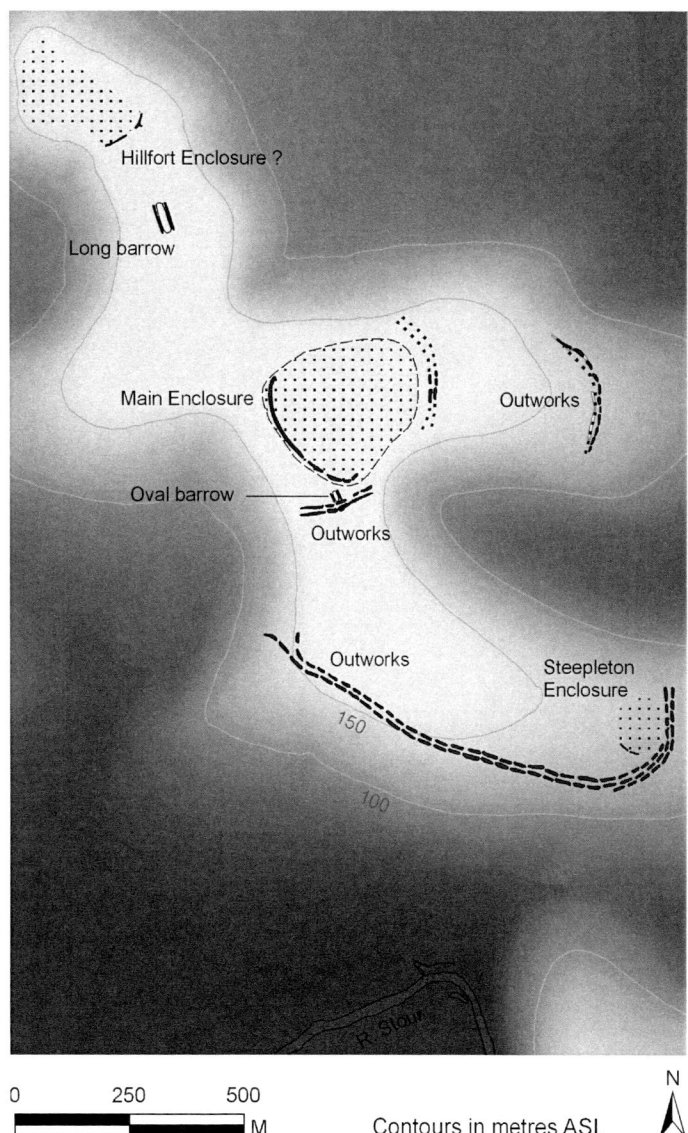

FIGURE 2. LOCATION OF THE ENCLOSURES AND LONG BARROWS ON HAMBLEDON HILL, DORSET. (FROM DARVILL 2010: FIGURE 48).

yet be determined, but on present evidence it seems more likely that a single enclosure was related to more than one long barrow. At Hambledon Hill, Dorset, at least two broadly contemporary causewayed enclosures are known on the top of a trefoil-shaped chalk upland (Figure 2). The main enclosure lies in the centre of hilltop and excavations between 1974 and 1986 showed that its ditches contained abundant disarticulated human remains; at least 11 adults and 19 immatures from the sample investigated (McKinley in Mercer and Healy 2008: 490). It is possible that some of these connect with burials made in a very large long barrow some 69 m long, 15 m wide, and 2.5 m high, that lies less than 500 m to the northwest. However, there are no recorded excavations of this monument so the links must remain speculative. By contrast, on the south side of the main enclosure there was a smaller oval-shaped barrow roughly 33 m by 15 m surrounded by a U-shaped segmented quarry ditch. When excavated this barrow was found to have been heavily disturbed, but displaced material included the remains of at least 4 adults and 1 immature that had probably come from a primary burial area in the central part of the mound (McKinley in Mercer and Healy 2008: 490). The main enclosure was constructed around 3680-3630 BC and continued in use for between 290 and 350 years. The oval barrow was constructed at the same time, 3680-3640 BC, and probably had a similar period of use (Bayliss *et al.* in Mercer and Healy 2008: Table 4.2).

The Cotswold Hills and adjacent upper Thames Valley continues the heavy concentration of long barrows and enclosures northwards from the chalklands of Wessex. Crickley Hill and the Peak Camp on the Cotswold escarpment overlooking the Severn Valley comprise a pair of enclosures less than 2 km apart whose histories are intertwined (Darvill 2011; Dixon 1988; Dixon *et al.* in Whittle *et al.* 2011: 434-465). A large long barrow at the Crippetts some 3 km north of Crickley Hill may connect with the community that used the Crickley enclosures but without excavation it is impossible to be sure (Figure 3). Rather more clear is the situation at the Peak Camp, first built around in 3650-3550 BC and refurbished on several successive occasions down to 3330-3215 BC (Bayliss *et al.* in Darvill

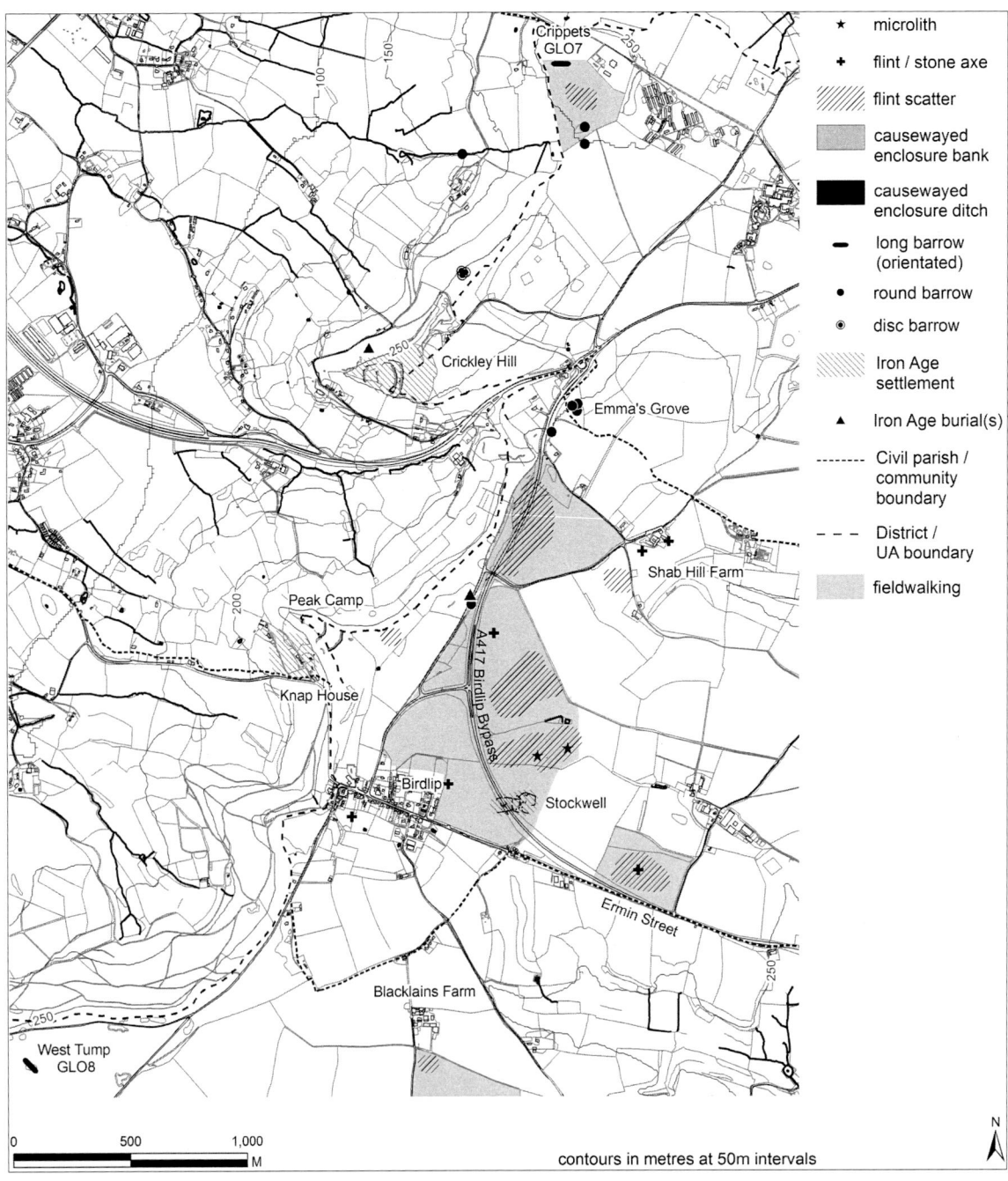

FIGURE 3. LOCATION OF CRICKLEY HILL AND THE PEAK CAMP ON THE COTSWOLD ESCARPMENT IN GLOUCESTERSHIRE WITH ADJACENT LONG BARROWS AND OTHER ARCHAEOLOGICAL FEATURES MARKED. (FROM DARVILL 2011: FIGURE 1).

2011: 187-194). Radiocarbon dates from burials at West Tump long barrow only half an hour's walk away from the Peak Camp to the south, span the period 3770-3630 BC to 3370-3090 BC (Smith and Brickley 2006: 340-343). This is more or less a mirror image of the Peak Camp range and it seems likely that the West Tump people were the builders, renovators, and users of Peak Camp.

Little is known about the relationships between the closely adjacent long barrows and enclosures at Adam's Grave and Knap Hill, Wiltshire (Cunnington 1912) and Roughton, Norfolk (Oswald et al. 2001: fig 6.7), but at Haddenham, Cambridgeshire, The Upper Delphs enclosure built 3820-2930 BC, probably towards the end of that period, seems to have been contemporary with the Foulmire Fen long barrow built in the mid fourth millennium BC just 3 km to the north (Evans and Hodder 2006; Whittle et al. 2011: 271-291).

Not all causewayed enclosures connect closely with adjacent barrows which is why understanding the chronology of monuments in a landscape context is so important. At Abingdon, Oxfordshire, for example the inner ditch of the well-known enclosure on the interfluve between two north-bank tributaries of the River Thames was constructed around 3655-3630 BC with the outer ditch dug soon afterwards around 3660-3620 BC (Avery 1982; Whittle et al. 2011: 418). This seems to be slightly earlier than the date of the burials from an oval barrow just outside the enclosure to the southeast that were deposited in the last third of the fourth millennium BC (Bradley 1992; Whittle et al. 2011: 429). However, there may be undated earlier phases to the barrow, and there are certainly other long barrows in the vicinity yet to be explored. Pit graves to the east of the Abingdon enclosure include at least one burial that is contemporary with the use of the enclosure (Barclay and Halpin 1999: 28-31) showing how important it is to build up a comprehensive picture of how landscapes were used through the fourth millennium BC.

Connections between enclosures and other types of burial monuments of the fourth millennium BC are poorly understood. Duggleby Howe, North Yorkshire, for example, is a large multi-phase round barrow whose burial sequence started about 3555-3415 BC with a shaft-grave. The mound was added in the twenty-ninth century BC. The surrounding ditch forming an enclosure 370 m in diameter with a wide entrance gap to the southeast is probably later still, having being constructed in the later third millennium BC (Gibson 2011: 39-40). In western England the hilltop enclosure at Helman Tor, Cornwall (Mercer 1997), lies 3 km southwest of Lesquite Quoit (Barnatt 1982: 136), but while the construction of the former can be dated to the period 3845-3650 BC (Whittle et al. 2011: 504) the portal dolmen at Lesquite remains undated and in a ruinous condition. Similarly, Carn Brea, Cornwall, constructed around 4040-3530 BC (Mercer 1981; Whittle et al. 2011: 509), could potentially overlap with the use of a nearby dolmen at Carnwynnen Quoit. But the latter collapsed in 1967 and has never been adequately excavated (Barnatt 1982: 135-136). Southwest Wales is much the same with the hilltop enclosure at Banc Du, Pembrokeshire, constructed 3645-3490 BC (Darvill et al. 2005: 22-23; Whittle et al. 2011: 526-527) but the small dolmen at Cerrig Lladron overlooking the site some 1.3 km to the northeast has never been excavated. In many parts of western Britain acidic soils mitigate against the preservation of bone so substantiating close associations between enclosures and burial places will always be difficult.

Pattern and purpose

Archaeological evidence coupled with detailed dating shows that, in many areas, enclosures were exactly contemporary with long barrows and various other kinds of burial monuments. Questions therefore focus on how these structures fitted together into wider patterns? And how were they bonded together through the lives lived out by those who built and used them? We will probably never know exactly how these things worked within such landscapes (but see Oswald et al. 2001: 114-119 for summary of attempts), but it is nevertheless worth attempting a general model which serves to illustrate the possibilities (cf. Darvill 2004: 200-213 for case study in the Cotswolds). Some of the main relevant strands of evidence have already been introduced, but in addition it is important to emphasize that the role of topography and environment are important considerations. No single model will fit all situations, although the size of populations, the number of sites used, and the scale of land-use may be more important than the fundamental articulations.

Variations in landscape type and environmental diversity are key factors that influence the nature and distribution of archaeological evidence throughout Britain, and both need to be taken into account. In topographic terms, Graeme Barker and Derek Webley have observed that many causewayed enclosures in southern Britain lie on or near the interface between contrasting environments (Barker and Webley 1978). In some cases the interface is between upland and valley land; in other cases it is between a river flood-plain and the raised terraces above. One implication throughout is that the populations who used these enclosures were in the optimum situation for the effective exploitation of a wide range of resources. Equally, the enclosures were optimally situated to bring together communities whose everyday existence focused on different environments and who might therefore make complementary contributions to the overall economy and the well-being of the community as a whole.

The idea that long barrows and enclosures were somehow central places in the lives of a community is widely held, but how this significance was realized has become a matter of considerable debate. For Colin Renfrew long barrows and various other kinds of contemporary monuments were the territorial markers of segmentary societies, constructed in a climate of social stress as pioneering farming communities filled the landscape and brought upon themselves increased competition for land and resources (Renfrew 1973). This is a theme that I developed with specific reference to the Cotswold-Severn region some years ago, arguing that architectural devices embedded in the design and construction of the long barrows provided a symbolic scheme that could be decoded by contemporary people to reveal information about identity, ownership, and control (Darvill 1982: 41-75). In such a scheme, communities occupied defined settlement areas for appreciable periods, in some cases constructing enclosures to contain and define their activities and act as foci for the living (cf. Fleming 1973). Such simple distinctions between settlements and ceremonial sites of the kind that seem obvious to us today do not really work for the kinds of small-scale societies that must be envisaged for early farming communities in Britain. Elman Service referred to such societies as 'tribes' – groups of families or clans who believe they have descended from common ancestors and who form a close-knit community under a defined leader (Service 1971: 99-132). The land occupied by such a group becomes a territory, perhaps physically subdivided and fractured along kinship lines. In such communities everyday life is shot through with what to modern eyes seem like strange patterns of behaviour involving degrees of reverence, taboo, and beliefs that transcend everything that is done; all of life in this sense is deeply embedded in the ideas that structure the way things are done (see Sahlins 1968: 96-113). Thus although communities live in one place and bury their dead somewhere else, these should not be seen as corresponding to our particular notions of ordered existence; rather, barrows and enclosures should be seen as nodal points in a scheme of the world which we have to try to understand in its own terms. Barrows and burial places may be central to one series of routines, perhaps at a local household scale, while enclosures were central to other spheres of activity, perhaps at an inter-community level.

The question of mobility, or the lack of it, is an important factor in thinking about the way monuments fit together and relate to each other. During the 1980s a model of early farming communities developed in which communities are seen as being highly mobile. In this view, long barrows and enclosures were fixed points in extensive patterns of movement, perhaps with communities periodically meeting together at large enclosures and visiting their ancestral barrows in the neighbourhood for ceremonies and the placement of human remains belonging to those who had died since the last visit. The monuments in this scheme become permanent nodes within an impermanent world. For John Barrett, 'the temporal and spatial referents of these lives would have been known in terms of the seasons and of the distances between places ... sites did not occupy the centers of territories so much as lie at the end of one path and the beginning of the next' (Barrett 1994: 141). Alasdair Whittle described this in terms of what he called 'tethered mobility', periodic returns to a small number of fixed points (1997: 21), while for Julian Thomas it was engagement in such mobility and the various cycles of movement that went with it, including seasonal movements from place to place, that contributed to the development of personhood – the quality or condition of being an individual (Thomas 1999: 228). It is a tempting and seductive model which by its nature requires relatively little archaeological evidence to support it. Indeed, it origins owe much to the apparent poverty of evidence for structures that could be considered as long-term houses or settlements (cf. Darvill and Thomas 1996). But so far as the fourth millennia BC in Britain as a whole is concerned there are certain difficulties with the peripatetic community model, not least the existence of fairly marked regional styles of material culture – pottery and long barrows are obvious cases – which at the very least suggest that perhaps the areas within which communities might have moved around were of fairly limited compass. In many areas, and southern Britain is certainly one, there is increasing evidence of more established settlement patterns, and, for a few centuries at least, a fairly static residence system.

Underlying many of these ideas is the presence of some kind of hierarchy in the connections between sites; certainly there are differences in the number of recorded examples of different kinds of site that may be relevant here. Although undoubtedly biased by the way that different kinds of site are recognized and brought to attention, the proportion of each is perhaps instructive: enclosures are the least numerous with long barrows about four times as common. Movements between these and other kinds of site were undoubtedly important, whether at the everyday level of farming and carrying on essential life-sustaining tasks, or through periodic visits to more distant places and the participation in less mundane activities.

Condensing out the archaeological patterns, it is possible to explore and illustrate the possibilities at two related scales, albeit in a very tentative and provisional way (Figure 4). At a general level, it can be suggested that sub-tribal communities occupy interlocking geographically definable areas or territories, the boundaries of which may be rather fuzzy but locally known to those who directly encounter them and their neighbours (Figure 4A). The notional centre of each territory would be an enclosure, some of which were permanently occupied, but all of which acted as periodic gathering places for the wider community. These enclosures were not necessarily in the geographical centre of the territory, but rather in convenient locations with good access to the range of environments accessible to the particular communities. Scattered around the territory there were other settlements, variously occupied on a permanent or temporary basis. Around the enclosures and the other settlements there would be long barrows, perhaps one for each local lineage or kinship group. Moving in closer to the more detailed scale of particular communities, the location and position of the enclosure, residential settlements, industrial areas, and barrows would have reflected sensitivity to the landscape, the local environment, and the extent of cleared land (Figure 4B). There is some reason to think that the barrows may have been on the edge of the cleared ground while the enclosures lay on or near the interface between critical environments. Trackways and paths connected the main elements in the settlement system, and in turn linked these with the wider environment and neighbouring communities.

Conclusion

Crude as they are in the light of available evidence, models of landscape organization help focus attention on what is known and how gaps in our knowledge about the lives of these communities might be filled. By the middle of the fourth millennium BC, long barrows were regularly constructed and used throughout southern Britain by communities who also built and used large earthwork enclosures for short-term and long-term occupation. In some cases they lived in small defended hilltop villages while elsewhere their long-houses were the focus of everyday routines. Ian Hodder has suggested that the physical separation that existed between the long barrows and the concentrations of habitation may have been part of the very changes in the way that people saw the world around them, and the reason that people built long barrows at all. He suggests that 'the drama of the control of nature would thus be enhanced by the very construction of the tomb in more distant and marginal

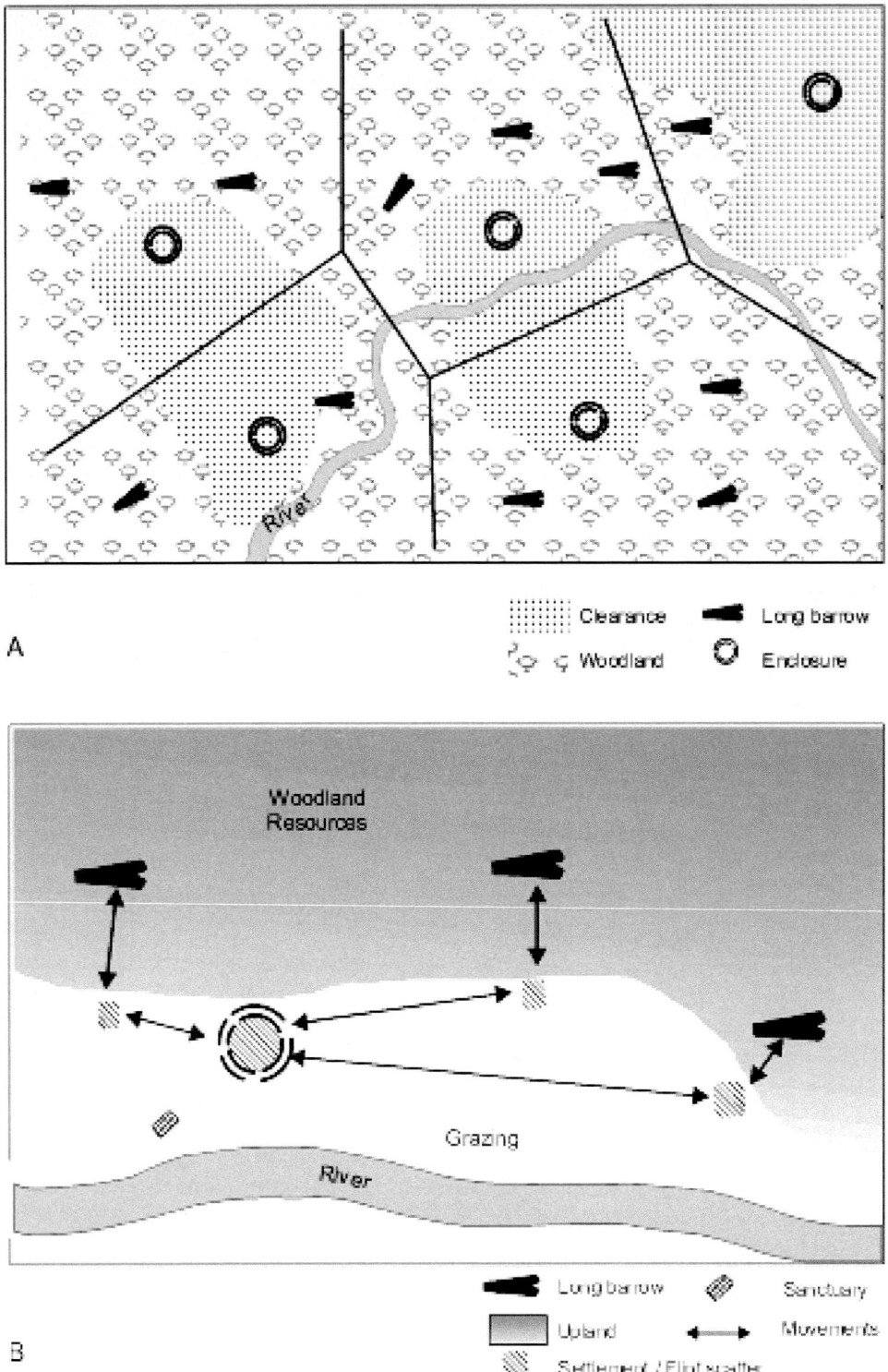

FIGURE 4. IDEALIZED SETTLEMENT PATTERN IN AREAS WITH LONG BARROWS AND ENCLOSURES. A. REGIONAL SYSTEM. B. LOCAL SYSTEM. (FROM DARVILL 2004: FIGURE 82).

places ... the gradual extension of the domus away from the domestic sphere' (Hodder 1990: 255). It is a powerful image and one that emphasises how important it is to situate and understand the formal and informal relationships between archaeologically visible monuments in the context of socially constructed space within a meaningfully constituted world that we can now only begin to glimpse.

Acknowledgements

Sections of this paper summarize and draw heavily on longer accounts of this topic published elsewhere (Darvill 2004: 187-213; 2010: 96-117). The illustrations were prepared by Vanessa Constant.

Bibliography

ASHBEE, P. 1969. Timber mortuary houses and earthen long barrows again. Antiquity. 43, p. 43-5.

ASHBEE, P. 1984. The earthen long barrow in Britain (Second edition). Norwich: Geo Books, 222 p.

AVERY, M. 1982. The Neolithic causewayed enclosure, Abingdon. In Case, H. J.; Whittle, A., eds. – Settlement patterns in the Oxford Region. London: Council for British Archaeology (Research Report 44), p. 19-50.

BARCLAY, A.; HALPIN, C. 1999. Excavations at Barrow Hills, Radley, Oxfordshire. Volume 1: The Neolithic and Bronze Age monument complex. Oxford: Oxford Archaeological Unit, 390 p.

BARKER, C. T. 1992. The chambered tombs of south-west Wales. Oxford: Oxbow Books (Monograph 14), 96 p.

BARKER, G.; WEBLEY, D. 1978. Causewayed camps and early Neolithic economies in central southern England. Proceedings of the Prehistoric Society. 44, p. 161-86.

BARNATT, J. 1982. Prehistoric Cornwall. The ceremonial monuments. Wellingborough: Turnstone Press.

BARRETT, J. C. 1994. Fragments from antiquity: an archaeology of social life in Britain, 2900-1200 BC. Oxford: Blackwell, 172 p.

BAYLISS, A.; WHITTLE, A. eds. 2007. Histories of the dead: building chronologies for five southern British long barrows. Cambridge Archaeological Journal. 17.1 (Supplement), p. 1-147.

BRADLEY, R. 1992. The excavation of an oval barrow beside the Abingdon causewayed enclosure, Oxfordshire. Proceedings of the Prehistoric Society. 58, 127-42.

BRADLEY, R. 1998. The significance of monuments. London: Routledge, 179 p.

CORCORAN, J. X. W. P. 1972. Multi-period construction and the origins of the chambered long cairn in western Britain and Ireland. In Lynch, F.; Burgess, C. eds. – Prehistoric man in Wales and the West. Bath: Adams and Dart, p. 31-64.

CUNNINGTON, M. E. 1912. Knap Hill Camp. Wiltshire Archaeological and Natural History Magazine. 37, p. 42-65.

CURWEN, E. C. 1930. Neolithic camps. Antiquity. 4, p. 22-54.

DANIEL, G. E. 1950. The prehistoric chamber tombs of England and Wales. Cambridge: At the University Press, 306 p.

DARVILL, T. 1982. The megalithic chambered tombs of the Cotswold-Severn region. Highworth: Vorda, 148 p.

DARVILL, T. 2004. Long barrows of the Cotswolds and surrounding areas. Stroud: Tempus, 320 p.

DARVILL, T. 2010. Prehistoric Britain (Second edition). Abingdon: Routledge, 416 p.

DARVILL, T. 2011. Excavations at a Neolithic enclosure on The Peak, near Birdlip, Gloucestershire. Proceedings of the Prehistoric Society. 77, p. 139-204.

DARVILL, T.; THOMAS, J. eds. 1996. Neolithic houses Northwest Europe and beyond. Oxford. Oxbow Books (Neolithic Studies Group Seminar Papers 1), 213 p.

DARVILL, T.; THOMAS, J. eds. 2001. Neolithic enclosures in Atlantic Northwest Europe. Oxford. Oxbow Books (Neolithic Studies Group Seminar Papers 6), 215 p.

DARVILL, T.; MORGAN EVANS, D.; FYFE, R.; WAINWRIGHT, G. 2005. Strumble-Preseli Ancient Communities and Environment Study (SPACES): Fourth report 2005. Archaeology in Wales. 45, p. 17-24.

DAVIDSON, J. L.; HENSHALL, A. S. 1989. The chambered cairns of Orkney. Edinburgh: Edinburgh University Press, 350 p.

DAVIDSON, J. L.; HENSHALL, A. S. 1991. The chambered cairns of Caithness. Edinburgh: Edinburgh University Press, 177 p.

DIXON, P. 1988. The Neolithic settlements on Crickley Hill. In Burgess, C.; Topping, P.; Mordant, C.; Maddison, M. eds. Enclosures and defences in the Neolithic of Western Europe. Oxford. British Archaeological Reports (BAR International Series 403. 2 vols), p. 75-88.

EVANS, C.; HODDER, I. 2006. A woodland archaeology. Neolithic sites at Haddenham. Cambridge: McDonald Institute Monographs, 262 p.

FLEMING, A. 1972. Vision and design: approaches to ceremonial monument typology. Man (NS). 7, p. 57-72.

FLEMING, A. 1973. Tombs for the living. Man (NS). 8, p. 177-93.

GIBSON, A. 2002. The late Neolithic palisaded enclosures of the United Kingdom. In Gibson, A. ed. – Behind wooden walls: Neolithic palisaded enclosures in Europe. Oxford: Archaeopress (BAR International Series 1013), p. 5-23.

GIBSON, A. 2011. Report on the excavation at the Duggleby Howe causewayed enclosure, North Yorkshire. Archaeological Journal. 168, p. 1-63.

HARDING, A. F.; LEE, G. E. 1987. Henge monuments and related sites of Great Britain. Air photographic evidence and catalogue. Oxford: British Archaeological Reports (BAR British Series 175).

HENSHALL, A. S. 1963. The chambered tombs of Scotland 1. Edinburgh: Edinburgh University Press, 456.

HENSHALL, A. S. 1972. The chambered tombs of Scotland 2. Edinburgh: Edinburgh University Press, 656 p.

HENSHALL, A. S.; RITCHIE, J. N. G. 1995. The chambered cairns of Sutherland. Edinburgh: Edinburgh University Press, 180 p.

HENSHALL, A. S.; RITCHIE, J. N. G. 2001. The chambered cairns of the Central Highlands. Edinburgh: Edinburgh University Press, 264 p.

HERITY, M. 1974. Irish passage graves. Dublin: Irish University Press, 308 p.

HODDER, I. 1990. The domestication of Europe. Structure and contingency in Neolithic societies. Oxford: Blackwell, 256 p.

KINNES, I. 1979. Round barrows and ring-ditches in the British Neolithic. London: British Museum (Occasional Paper 7).

KINNES, I. 1992. Non-megalithic long barrows and allied structures in the British Neolithic. London: British Museum (Occasional Paper 52).

KLASSEN, L. 2014. Along the road. Aspects of causewayed enclosures in southern Scandinavia and beyond. Aarhus: Aarhus University Press, 330 p.

KYTMANNOW, T. 2008. Portal tombs in the landscape. The chronology, morphology and landscape setting of the portal tombs of Ireland, Wales and Cornwall. Oxford: BAR (British Series 455), 210 p.

LEARY, J.; DARVILL, T.; FIELD, D., eds. 2010. Round mounds and monumentality in the British Neolithic and beyond. Oxford: Oxbow Books (Neolithic Studies Group Seminar Papers 10), 256 p.

LYNCH, F. M. 1975. Carreg Samson megalithic tomb, Mathry, Pembrokeshire. Archaeologia Cambrensis. 124, p. 15-35.

LYNCH, F. 1976. Towards a chronology of megalith tombs in Wales. In Boon, G. C; Lewis, J. M. eds. – Welsh Antiquity. Cardiff. National Museum of Wales, p. 63-79.

MADSEN, T. 1979. Earthen long barrows and timber structures: aspects of the early Neolithic mortuary practice in Denmark. Proceedings of the Prehistoric Society. 45, p. 301-20.

MERCER, R. 1981. Excavations at Carn Brea, Illogan, Cornwall, 1970-73. Cornish Archaeology. 20, p. 1-204.

MERCER, R. 1997. The excavation of a Neolithic enclosure complex at Helman Tor, Lostwithiel, Cornwall. Cornish Archaeology. 36, p. 5-64.

MERCER, R; HEALY, F. 2008. Hambledon Hill, Dorset, England. Excavation and survey of a Neolithic monument complex and its surrounding landscape. London: English Heritage (2 vols), 816 p.

MICHELL, J. 1982. Megalithomania. Artists, antiquarians and archaeologists at the old stone monuments. London: Thames and Hudson, 168 p.

OSWALD, A.; DYER, C.; BARBER, M. 2001. The creation of Monuments. Neolithic causewayed enclosures in the British Isles. London: English Heritage, 200 p.

PALMER, R. 1976. Interrupted ditch enclosures in Britain: the use of aerial photography for comparative studies. Proceedings of the Prehistoric Society. 42, p. 161-86.

PHILP, B.; DUTTO, M. 1985. The Medway megaliths (Second edition). Dover: Kent Archaeological Trust, 16 p.

PIGGOTT, S. 1954. The Neolithic cultures of the British Isles. Cambridge: At the University Press, 420 p.

PIGGOTT, S. 1962. The West Kennet Long Barrow. Excavations 1955-56. London: HMSO, 16 p. (Ministry of Works Archaeological Reports 4).

POWELL, T. G. E.; CORCORAN, J. X. W. P.; LYNCH, F.; SCOTT, J. G. 1969. Megalithic enquiries in the west of Britain. Liverpool: Liverpool University Press, 357 p.

RENFREW, C. 1973. Monuments, mobilization and social organization in Neolithic Wessex. In Renfrew, C. ed. – The explanation of culture change. London: Duckworth, p. 539-58.

SAHLINS, M. D. 1968. Tribesmen. Englewood Cliffs: Prentice-Hall, 118 p.

SERVICE, E. R. 1971. Primitive social organization: an evolutionary perspective (Second edition). New York: Random House, 221 p.

SHERIDAN, A.; SCHULTING, R.; QUINNELL, H.; TAYLOR, R. 2008. Revisiting a small passage tomb at Broadsands, Devon. Proceedings of the Devon Archaeological Society. 66, p. 1-26.

SMITH, I. F. 1965. Windmill Hill and Avebury. Excavations by Alexander Keiller 1925-1939. Oxford. Clarendon Press, 265 p.

SMITH, I. F.; EAGLES, B.; BOWEN, H. C. 1979. Long barrows in Hampshire and the Isle of Wight. London: RCHME, 114 p.

SMITH, M.; BRICKLEY, M. 2006. The date and sequence if use of Neolithic funerary monuments: new AMS dating evidence from the Cotswold-Severn region. Oxford Journal of Archaeology. 25:4, p. 335-56.

THOMAS, J. 1999. Understanding the Neolithic. London: Routledge, 266 p.

THORPE, N. 1984. Ritual, power and ideology: a reconstruction of earlier Neolithic rituals in Wessex. In Bradley, R.; Gardiner, J. eds. – Neolithic studies. A review of some current research. Oxford: British Archaeological Reports (BAR British Series 133), p. 41-60.

WHITTLE, A. 1991. Wayland's Smithy, Oxfordshire: excavations at the Neolithic tomb in 1962-63 by R. J. C. Atkinson and S. Piggott. Proceedings of the Prehistoric Society. 57:2, p. 61-102.

WHITTLE, A. 1997. Moving on and moving around: Neolithic settlement mobility. In Topping, P. ed. – Neolithic landscapes. Oxford: Oxbow Books (Neolithic Studies Group Seminar Papers 2), p. 15-22.

WHITTLE, A.; HEALY, F.; BAYLISS, A. 2011. Gathering time. Dating the early Neolithic enclosures of Southern Britain and Ireland. Oxford: Oxbow Books, 992 p.

WHITTLE, A.; POLLARD, J.; GRIGSON, C. 1999. The harmony of symbols. The Windmill Hill causewayed enclosure, Wiltshire. Oxford. Oxbow Books, 404 p.

House and megalith. Some remarks on the Niedźwiedź type tombs in the Eastern group of the TRB culture

Seweryn RZEPECKI
Institute of Archaeology, University of Łódź, ul. Uniwersytecka 3, Łódź, 91-404, Poland
rzepecki@uni.lodz.pl

Abstract

The aim of this article is to present views for the origin of Niedźwiedź type tombs in the Eastern group of the TRB culture. The characteristics of these structures include: the presence of a foundation trench in which a wooden palisade or wattle-work structure was originally located, the frequent lack of unambiguous burial traces and a lack of earthen mounds. Other characteristics of these structures such as: orientation, a trapezoid or elongated shape clearly refer to all the long tombs of the TRB culture. The author presents the context of the Niedźwiedź type tombs occurrence. At the same time, he indicates two fundamental sources of inspiration which potentially may have been responsible for their genesis.

Keywords: *TRB culture, megaliths, Niedźwiedź type tombs*

Résumé

Le but de cet article est de présenter les idées sur les tombes mégalithiques de type Niedźwiedź. Ces tombes sont associées à la culture des Gobelets en Entonnoir (TRB). Leurs caractéristiques sont: tranchée de fondation, où était jadis implantée la palissade en bois ou la construction en torchis, absence fréquente de traces de sépultures et absence de tertre. Les autres caractéristiques des ces structures, telles que l'orientation, la forme trapézoïdale ou allongée, se réfèrent à l'ensemble des tombes allongées de la culture des Gobelets en Entonnoir. Selon l'opinion de l'auteur, les tombes de type Niedźwiedź sont apparues sur le territoire des Plaines Polonaises comme élément d'un ensemble plus vaste de caractéristiques (vases en forme d'entonnoir, discques de terre cuite, sépultures en position verticale, petites maisons sur poteaux) associées à l'influence des cultures Cerny et Michelsberg.

Mots-clés: *Culture des Gobelets en Entonnoir (TRB), mégalithes, sépultures de type Niedźwiedź, Plaines Polonaises*

Introduction

To indicate the most important 'critical points' of the early (5450-4400 BC) and middle (4400-3650 BC) Neolithic of central Europe attention should be paid to the processes generating the occurrence of two cultures: the Linear Band Pottery culture (LBK) and the Funnel Beaker culture (TRB). The former initiated the use of enclaves of soils with the highest agricultural values, whereas the latter – enlarged the extent of agriculture with areas nowadays covered with poor-quality podsols (e.g. Czerniak 1988; Rzepecki 2004; Nowak 2009). Historical significance of both processes is evident, it is however worth paying attention to a certain structural difference. The LBK colonization and development of Danubian groups were accompanied by gradual divergence of initial homogeneity of architectural, sepulchral, economic norms as well as these concerning pottery-making, tool production, etc. On the other hand, the TRB culture was formed by a process of convergence. Individual societies joined the 'funnel beaker world' maintaining, in many cases for whole centuries, particular economic, architectonic and funeral patterns (cf. Zapotocky 1986, 1992; Lichardus 1991; Czerniak and Kośko 1993; Rzepecki 2004, 2011a). From this perspective the TRB genesis ceased to be a one-off event of precise localization – but it became a process of a spread and flow of ideas for which vessels in the shape of a funnel beaker, battle axes (Zapotocky 1992) as well as megalithic tombs were symbols. The following text concentrates on a problem of the occurrence of hypothetically the earliest form of the Eastern TRB group tombs which occupied the area of the Polish Lowlands – the so-called Niedźwiedź type tombs are concerned here (Fig. 1).

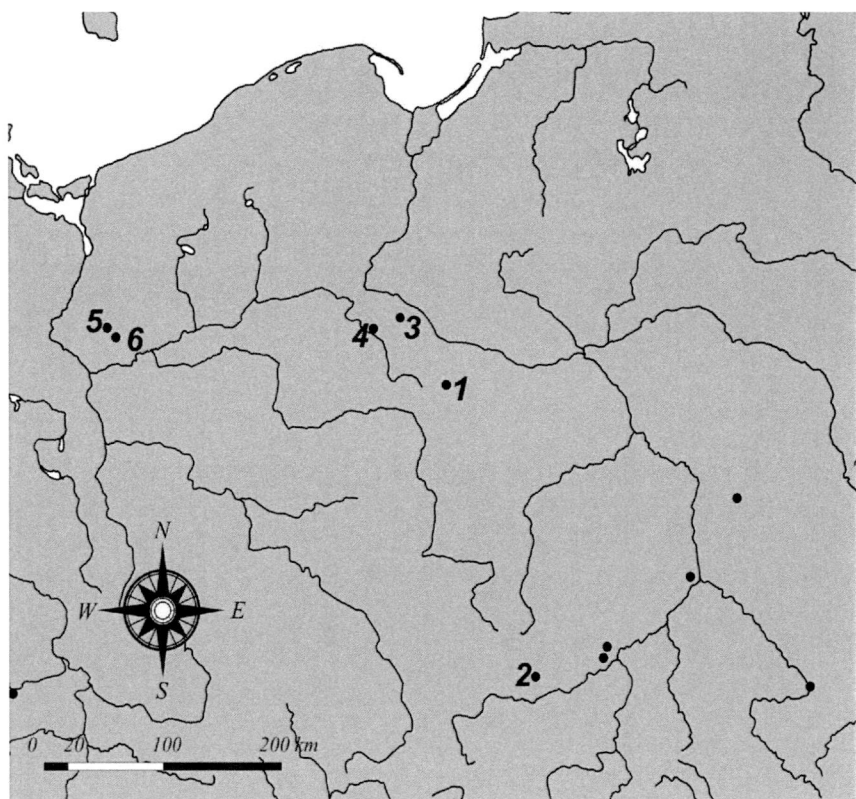

FIGURE 1. DISTRIBUTION OF THE NIEDŹWIEDŹ TYPE TOMBS IN POLAND.
SITES MENTIONED IN TEXT: 1 – SARNOWO 1; 2 – NIEDŹWIEDŹ 1; 3 – PODGAJ 7A;
4 – INOWROCŁAW 95; 5 – RENICE 5/6; 6 – JASTRZĘBIEC 4.

1. Sarnowo and Niedźwiedź. A megalith and a 'house'

In the 1960s and 1970s research works at two sites from distant regions of Poland were almost simultaneously carried out. Lidia Gabałówna and Henryk Wiklak – students of Professor Konrad Jażdżewski investigated tombs no. 7, 8, and 9 at the site of Sarnowo 1, (Wiklak 1980, 1986). It is worth a brief reminder that these were monumental long tombs (up to c. 80 m long) with earthen mounds and stone kerbs. The buried – in the main burials they were mostly males – were deposited in a supine position (Midgley 1985). A good example of such type of 'classical' form of megalith is, for instance, tomb 8 from Sarnowo (Fig. 2: C). Its extent is determined by the course of irregular, 'blurred' contours which are traces of stone embankment – excavated at the beginning of the 20th century. On these grounds, it can be thought that the monument was oriented ENE-WSW. Its length was 71 m, with the width of the base c. 12 m. The central grave was discovered 12 m from the east edge of the structure. It was formed by a rectangular stone pavement. Although no traces of skeleton were discovered, an arrangement of the grave pit (2.4 x 0.9 m) indicates that the dead was deposited on their backs. The other two graves, containing the remains of a female (aged 18) and a male (aged 40-50) were registered within an 'annexe' – slightly younger, attached part of the tomb. What is interesting, is the tomb itself was located on the site of an older settlement – its remains are pit no. 1 and a cultural layer.

What should be emphasised is the significance of the 'means of expression' used to construct the 'classical' Kuyavian barrows (of the Sarnowo type). The tombs were equipped with solid stone kerbs and high earthen embankments. It was probably imposed by a desire to immortalise the memory of the buried ancestors. As a result, they became one of the most permanent elements of the cultural landscape of the Polish Lowland. Researchers of megaliths also experienced their suggestiveness.

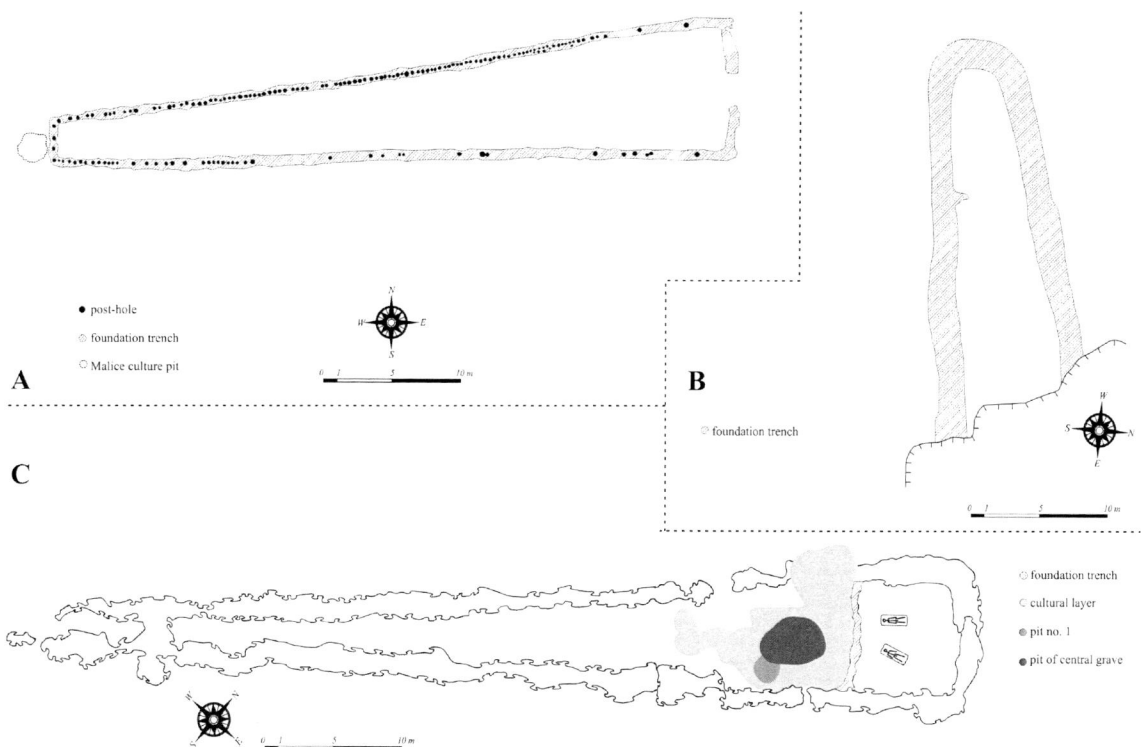

FIGURE 2. SARNOWO AND NIEDŹWIEDŹ TYPE TOMBS. A – NIEDŹWIEDŹ 1; B – PODGAJ 7A;
C – SARNOWO 1, TOMB 8 (AFTER RZEPECKI 2011, 2014).

Therefore, there is nothing peculiar about the fact that tombs differing from the 'Sarnowo norm' were defined as 'degenerated' (Jażdżewski 1973).

In the years 1967-1973 research at the site of Niedźwiedź 1 was also in progress (Burchard 1973; Rzepecki 2011, 2013, 2014). A structure in the shape of a trapeze oriented E-W was discovered at the site. It was 48 m long, 9.5 m wide at the base and about 3.2 m wide at the top. The trapeze formed a foundation trench 0.5-0.7 m wide and 0.7 m deep (Fig. 1: A). Within it 150 post-holes were recognized. It should be added that the exploration of the trench itself did not yield any pottery material allowing for the structure to be dated. In such a situation Burchard paid attention to a pit located next to the western edge of the feature; it yielded pottery of the Malice culture. On these grounds the discovery from Niedźwiedź spread in scientific literature as an example of a house of the Danubian people. This view was questioned by Magdalena Midgley (1985) who indicated similarities between the feature and the tradition of the TRB culture long tombs. In my works the tomb from Niedźwiedź gave a name to a specific type of the TRB culture monuments (Rzepecki 2011a, 2011b, 2013, 2014).

The problems connected with the recognition of the functions of Niedźwiedź features are, in my opinion, of archetypic significance for considerations on the origin of this type of tomb. I will return to this issue further on in the paper.

2. Niedźwiedź type tombs in the Eastern TRB: a review

From the area of the Eastern group of the TRB five sites with Niedźwiedź type tombs are known (Fig. 1-3), these are: Podgaj 7A, Inowrocław 95, Jastrzębiec 4, Renice 5-6, and Sarnowo 1 (Wiklak 1980; Czerniak and Kośko 1993; Rzepecki 2011a, 2014).

The site of Podgaj 7A was excavated at the turn of the 1970s. At that time, only a partly preserved monument oriented on the line E-W (Fig. 2: B) was registered. The foundation trench was visible on the length of c. 23 m, the width of the monument should be estimated at 7.5-10 m. Within the trench abundant TRB pottery material and considerable amounts of bones, mostly cattle, were discovered. At first, the feature was interpreted as a relic of a house, later only as a tomb (Czerniak and Kośko 1993; Rzepecki 2004, 2011a). It should be added that it was located on an older settlement of the TRB population.

Similar doubts concerning the features functions accompanied research at site Inowrocław 95. On the area of c. 1.3 ha it yielded evident traces of the TRB campsites on which funeral features 'overlapped'. They included 8 flat graves, with supine position of the bodies, 1 stone tomb and 3 Niedźwiedź type structures. They were very poorly preserved, their length probably did not exceed several metres. All sepulchral features of the TRB formed a vast complex which, on the grounds of radiocarbon dating from the flat graves, can be dated to a period 4000-3400 BC (Czerniak and Kośko 1993; Rzepecki 2011a).

A very similar situation as in Inowrocław 95 was registered on a cemetery at Jastrzębiec 4. On the area of c. 1.5 ha older traces of the TRB population campsites and 11 Niedźwiedź type tombs (Fig. 3: A) were discovered. Most of these structures were oriented N-S. Their length ranged from 4 to c. 13 m, within some of them hypothetical grave pits were registered. Radiocarbon dates obtained from animal bones discovered in the trenches oscillate between 3700-3000 BC (Rzepecki 2011a, 2011b).

Three monuments, including a 'doubled' one, were identified at the site of Renice 5-6. Their preserved lengths range from 13-34 m, with the width of c. 6-12 m (Fig. 3: B). Likewise the before described features were located on an area of an older settlement of the TRB culture. The tombs themselves were accompanied by ritual features connected with the consumption and burials of animal remains. Radiocarbon indications date these features to a period 3800-3700 BC (Rzepecki 2011a, 2011b).

At this point it is necessary to return to the discoveries made within tomb 8 in Sarnowo. Discoveries made there have lately been reinterpreted (Rzepecki 2014). Everything seems to indicate that the tomb had a form known from Niedźwiedź. The only evidence of its existence is a transverse foundation trench recognized in the tomb base zone (Rzepecki 2014). It avoided destruction during the rearrangement of the monument. The wooden palisade was at that time replaced with a stone kerb, the monument was extended eastwards by building a so-called 'annexe', and the tomb was equipped with an earthen mound. It was accompanied by the deposition of two burials, previously mentioned (Fig. 2: C).

2.1. Summarizing description

At this point it is worth summarizing the above information. All presented tombs were erected on an area that was earlier settled by the TRB societies. What they have in common is the use of wooden posts or 'lighter' wattle-work structures placed in foundation trenches. The latter formed trapezes (Fig. 2: B) or ovals (Fig. 3); sometimes the trench lines were interrupted by what clearly appears to be the location of an entrance. A good example is tomb D145 from Jastrzębiec 4 (Fig. 3: A). Structures of such a type from the area of the Eastern TRB were most often not of huge sizes. In most cases their length did not exceed 30 m. Usually, they did not contain grave pits or earthen mounds filling the space between the palisade lines. The dead were probably laid in a supine position. This is indicated by both traits of the hypothetical grave pits (e.g. tomb C297 from Jastrzębiec 4, Sarnowo 1 – the central grave), and the visible regionalism of patterns of laying the dead within Niedźwiedź type tombs – each time the norms refer to the traditions of the TRB local groups (Rzepecki 2011a). Interesting data was also provided by the reinterpretation of a famous tomb no. 8 from Sarnowo 1 (Rzepecki 2014). This monument indicates not only the functional integrability of the debated structures with other forms of the TRB monumental funerary architecture. First of all, it clearly locates the tradition of the palisade graves at the roots of Megalithism in the Polish Lowlands. They became direct patterns for slightly later forms of tombs known, among others, from Sarnowo.

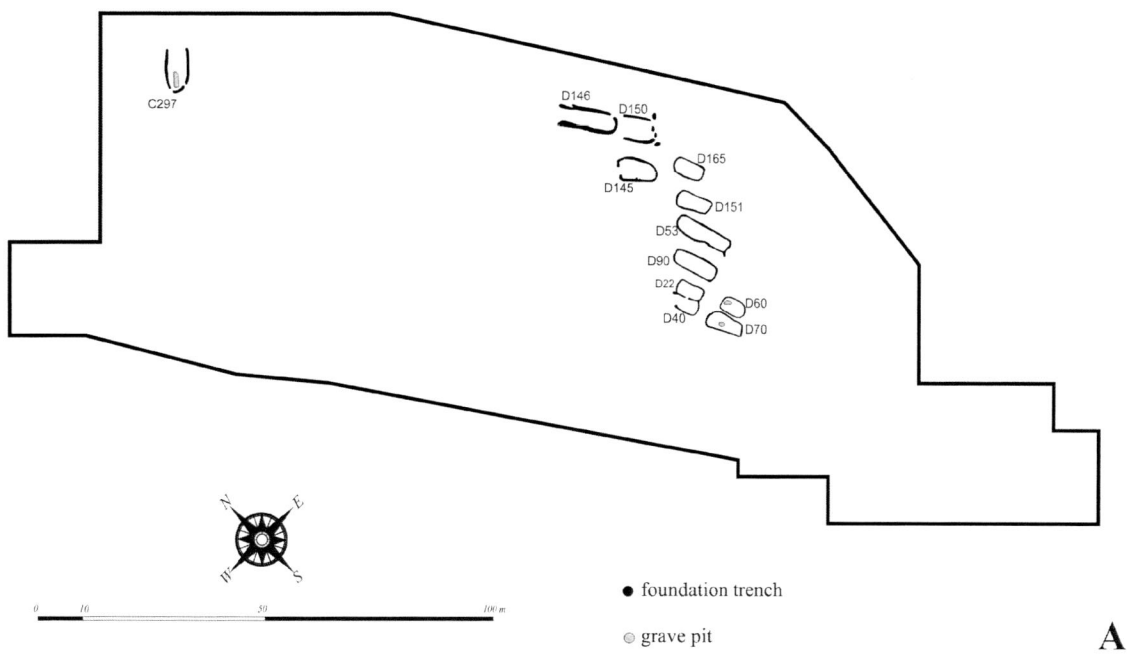

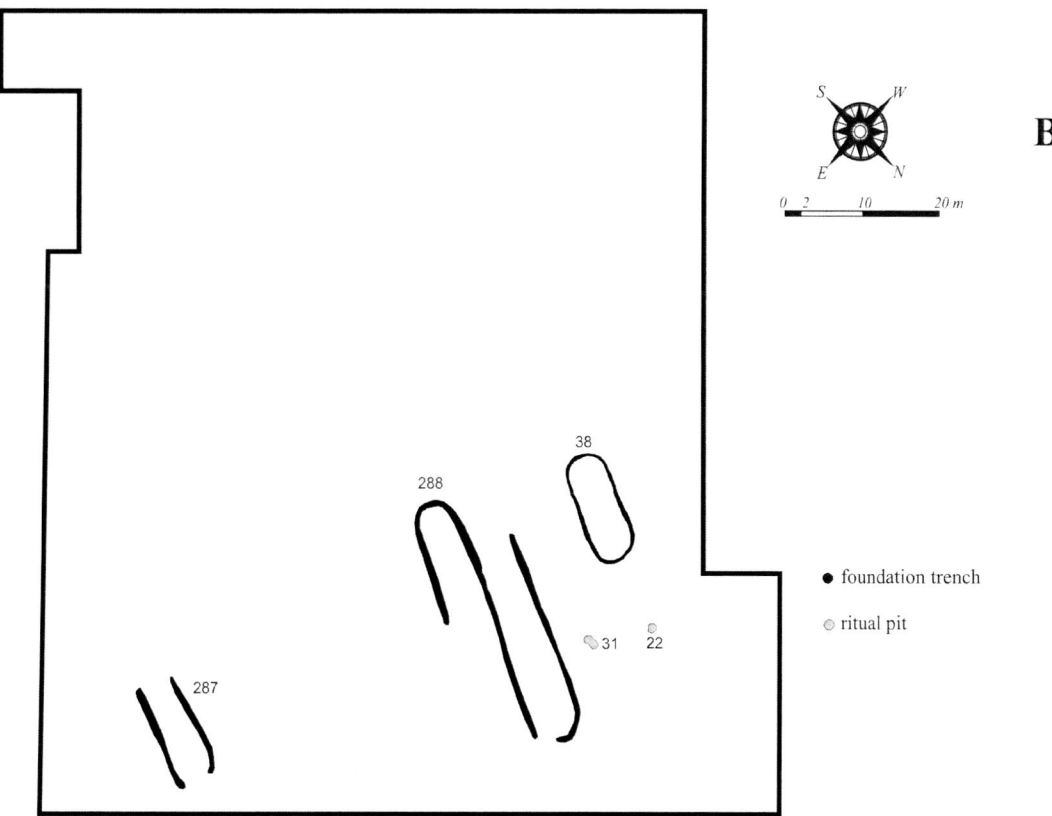

Figure 3. Niedźwiedź type tombs. A – Jastrzębiec 4; B – Renice 5/6 (after Rzepecki 2011).

As it was reasoned above, relations between 'classical' (e.g. Sarnowo) forms of Kuyavian barrows and Niedźwiedź type tombs are full of ambivalence. Both types are very similar in shape and are similarly oriented. Whereas, the fundamental differences concern the arrangement and durability of the structures. In the case of tombs known from, among others, Sarnowo it was intentionally aimed at a kind of protection of the dead body. The remains were deposited in grave pits or in stone kerbs.

The above mentioned desire to immortalise the memory of the dead also imposed an impressive and permanent structural approach (the use of stone and earthen embankments). The situation is different as far as Niedźwiedź type tombs are concerned. The dead bodies were probably laid directly on the surface. At the same time, no earth was used to construct the embankments and stones to arrange the kerbs. This obviously was not conductive to the preservation of the remains within such kinds of structures. On the other hand, wooden palisades or wattle-work were placed in foundation trenches. The durability of such structures was of course incomparably shorter than in the case of 'classical' Kuyavian barrows. They, however, had one important positive feature – in a mimetic way they imitated houses of the Danubian societies. This idea will be developed further on.

3. Niedźwiedź type tombs: looking for their origin

The similarity of the structure discovered in Niedźwiedź to the houses of the Danubian societies is beyond any doubts. For a full understanding of further analysis a small digression is necessary.

The middle Neolithic (c. 4400-3650 BC) in the Polish Lowlands was a scene of contemporaneous existence of two agricultural societies. The Brześć Kujawski culture (BKC) has older, Danubian roots. Societies which it included maintained traditions of their direct ancestors (LBK). They inhabited the most fertile soils, built long houses and established small cemeteries within their yards. The dead were deposited in a contracted position, and their graves sometimes were abounded in numerous copper ornaments. Beside – sometimes in a topographic sense – the oldest societies of the Eastern TRB existed. They occupied poor sandy soils, establishing settlements built-up with small rectangular houses. As I mentioned before, the TRB societies preferred depositing their dead on the areas of former settlements, in supine position. The graves are seldom equipped, whereas part of the dead (leaders) were laid within the above described Niedźwiedź and Sarnowo type tombs (Rzepecki 2015).

Let us return to the main theme of the analysis. Since the 1930s numerous houses of the BKC with constructions similar to Niedźwiedź type tombs are known (Fig. 4: A). It is now worth mentioning one of V. G. Childe's works (1949). According to him, linear TRB tombs were the effects of a desire to imitate Danubian structures. To evidence this thesis he used the results of research from Brześć Kujawski (Grygiel 1986). This idea was also developed by Ian Hodder (1984: 54-60, 1990: 145-147), Andrew Sherratt (1990, 1999), Richard Bradley (1998) and Magdalena Midgley (2005). Sherratt (1990) explicitly emphasized a possibility of a local, independent, from western Europe, genesis of long tombs centered in the Polish Lowlands. Niedźwiedź type tombs in such interpretations would be an imitation of houses or ruins of houses of the BKC societies (Fig. 4: B).

In my opinion, the issue of the occurrence of Niedźwiedź type tombs should be considered in context of the whole of the characteristics of the early TRB materials. What is also worth mentioning is the pottery traditions: the predominance of poorly decorated funnel beakers and plates (clay discs) decorated with fingerprints. None of the characteristics can be derived from the BKC environment (Larsson and Rzepecki 2003; Rzepecki 2004, 2011a) and the sources for a complex of early TRB traits should be searched for among societies of the West. I locate the epicentre zone for these traditions in the area of the Paris Basin. Among the Cerny culture societies all key elements for the early TRB (funnel beakers, clay discs, burials in straight position, small post houses), and first of all, tombs of the Passy type (Delor *et al.* 1997; Duhamel *et al.* 1997) can be found. Characteristics of their construction and orientation are forecasts of the arrangements known from Niedźwiedź type tombs. An important stage of proliferation of the Cerny culture traditions was the emergence of the Michelsberg culture (cf. Jeunesse *et al.* 2004; Jeunesse 2010). To say nothing about the pottery traits, attention should be paid to the tomb discoveries from sites Beaurieux, Vignely, Saint-Julien-du-Salt,

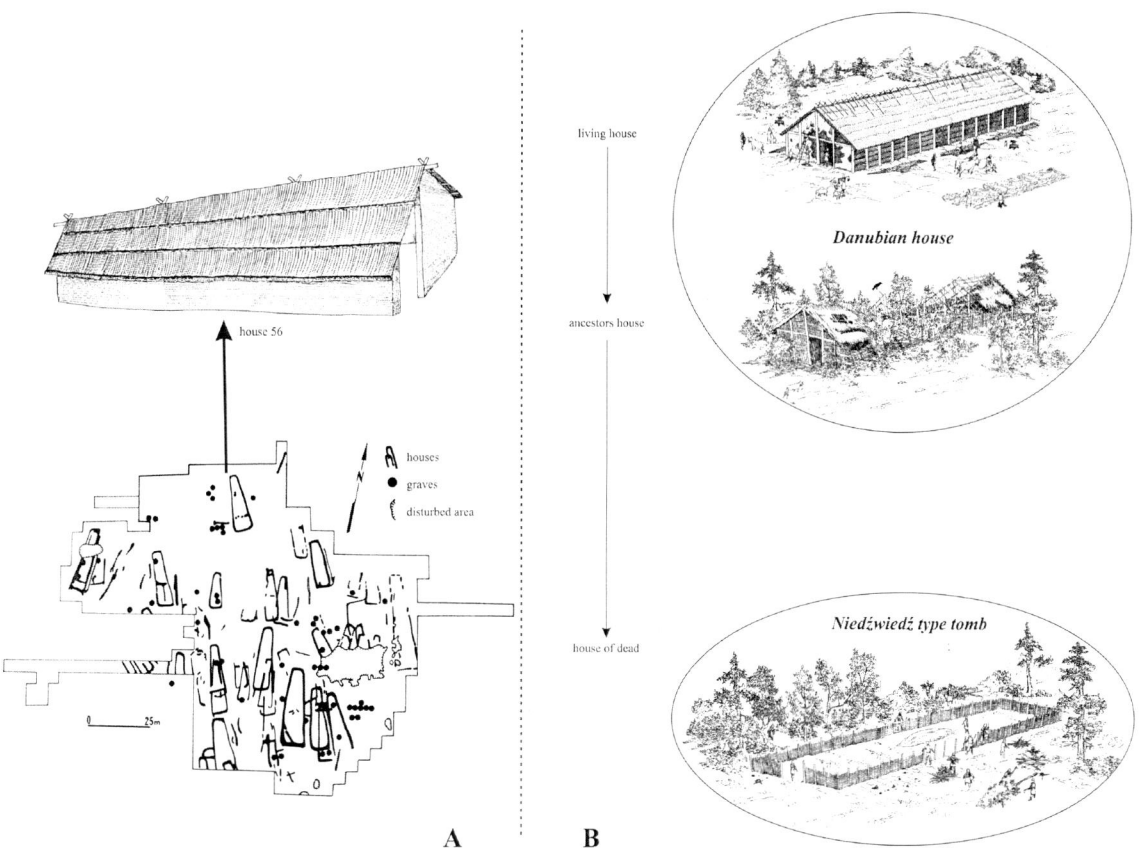

FIGURE 4. DANUBIAN HOUSES AND NIEDŹWIEDŹ TYPE TOMBS. A – PLAN OF THE SETTLEMENT AND CEMETERY AT BRZEŚĆ KUJAWSKI 4 AND RECONSTRUCTION OF HOUSE 56 (AFTER GRYGIEL 1986); B – TRANSFORMATION OF THE IDEA OF DANUBIAN LONG HOUSES INTO NIEDŹWIEDŹ TYPE TOMBS (AFTER RZEPECKI 2011).

Bochum-Hiltrop, Padeborn-Saatental, Friedberg (Chambon and Lanchon 2003; Colas *et al.* 2007; Thévenet 2007; Schade-Lindig 2008; Knoche 2008; Gronenborn 2010).

A fragment of the phenomenon of the Cerny culture patterns penetration eastwards was the occurrence of Niedźwiedź type tombs in the Polish Lowlands. They were accompanied by an 'invasion' of other traits of western European provenance (Rzepecki 2011a). In the context of the developing societies of the BKC, the contents hidden behind Niedźwiedź type tombs were partially transformed. They not only became a symbolic surrogate of long houses. Their mimetism in relation to the 'Danubian' buildings also enabled a direct affirmation of the cult of the ancestors. This phenomenon set a framework for the 'confrontation' of the TRB and BKC and definitely determined the TRB culture success (Rzepecki 2015).

Bibliography

BRADLEY, R. 1998. The Significance of Monuments. On the shaping of human experience in Neolithic and Bronze Age Europe. London and New York: Routledge, 179 p.

BURCHARD, B. 1973. Z badań neolitycznej budowli trapezowatej w Niedźwiedziu, pow. Miechów/stan. 1. Sprawozdania Archeologiczne. Kraków. 25, p. 39-48.

CHAMBON, P.; LANCHON, Y. 2003. Les structures sépulcrales de la nécropole de Vignely (Seine-et-Marne). Mémoire de la Société préhistorique Française. Paris. 33, p. 159-173.

CHILDE, V. G. 1949. The Origin of the Neolithic Culture in Northern Europe. Antiquity. 23, p. 129-135.

CHMIELEWSKI, W. 1952. Zagadnienie grobowców kujawskich w świetle ostatnich badań. Łódź: Wydawnictwo Muzeum Archeologicznego, 109 p.

COLAS, C.; BAILLIEU, M.; NAZE, Y. 2007. Un bâtiment monumental Cerny à Beaurieux 'la Plaine' (Aisne): présentation préliminaire. Interneo. Paris. 7, p. 59-69.

CZERNIAK, L. 1988. Czynniki zewnętrzne w rozwoju kulturowym społeczeństw Kujaw w okresie wczesnego i środkowego neolitu. In Cofta-Broniewska A. ed. Kontakty pradziejowych społeczeństw Kujaw z innymi ludami Europy. Studia do dziejów Kujaw 2. Inowrocław: Urząd Miejski w Inowrocławiu, p. 55-79.

CZERNIAK, L.; KOŚKO, A. 1993. Z badań nad genezą i systematyką kultury pucharów lejkowatych na Kujawach. Poznań: Uniwersytet im. Adama Mickiewicza w Poznaniu, 172 p.

DELOR, J.-P.; GENREAU, F.; HEURTAUX, A.; JACOB, J.-P.; LEREDDE, H.; NOUVEL, P.; PELLET, C. 1997. L'implantation des nécropoles monumentales au sud du Bassin parisien. In Constantin, C.; Mordant, D.; Simonin, D. eds. – La Culture de Cerny. Nouvelle économie, nouvelle société au Néolithique. Nemours: Mémoires du Musée de Préhistoire d'Île-de-France. 6, p. 381-395.

DUHAMEL, P.; FONTON, M.; CARRÉ, H. 1997. La nécropole monumentale de Passy (Yonne): description d'ensemble et problèmes d'interprétation. In Constantin, C.; Mordant, D.; Simonin, D. eds. – La Culture de Cerny. Nouvelle économie, nouvelle société au Néolithique. Nemours: Mémoires du Musée de Préhistoire d'Île-de-France. 6, p. 397-448.

GRONENBORN, D. 2010. Eliten, Prestigegüter, Repräsentationsgräber. Eine Spurensuche nach politischen Organisationsformen. In Jungsteinzeit im Umbruch. Die 'Michelsberger Kultur' und Mitteleuropa vor 6000 Jahren, Karlsruhe: Badisches Landesmuseum, p. 243-249.

GRYGIEL, R. 1986. The household cluster as a fundamental social unit of the Lengyel Culture in the Polish Lowlands. Prace i Materiały Muzeum Archeologicznego i Etnograficznego w Łodzi. Łódź. 31, 43-334.

HODDER, I. 1990. The Domestication of Europe. Oxford: Basil Blackwell, 331 p.

HODDER, I. 1984. Burials, women and men in the European Neolithic. In Miller, D.; Tilley, C., eds. – Ideology, Power and Prehistory. Cambridge: Cambridge University Press, p. 51-68

JAŻDŻEWSKI, K. 1936. Kultura pucharów lejkowatych w Polsce Zachodniej i Środkowej. Poznań: Biblioteka Prahistoryczna, 457 p.

JAŻDŻEWSKI, K. 1973. The Relations between Kujavian Barrows in Poland and Megalithic Tombs in northern Germany, Denmark and Western European Countries. In Daniel, G.; Kjærum, P. eds. – Megalithic Graves and Ritual, Papers presented at the III Atlantic Colloquium, Moesgård (1969): Jutland Archaeological Society, Publications XI. København, p. 63-74.

JEUNESSE, C. 2010. Die Michelsberger Kultur. In Jungsteinzeit im Umbruch. Die 'Michelsberger Kultur' und Mitteleuropa vor 6000 Jahren, Karlsruhe: Badisches Landesmuseum, p. 46-55.

JEUNESSE, C.; LEFRANC, P.; DENAIRE, A. 2004. Groupe de Bischheim, origine du Michelsberg, genèse du groupe d'Entzheim. La transition entre Néolithique moyen et le Néolithique récent dans les régions rhénanes. Zimmersheim. Cahiers de l'Association pour la Promotion de la Recherche Archéologique en Alsace. Tomes 18/19 (2002/2003), 281 p.

KNOCHE, B. 2008. Die Erdwerke von Soest (Kr. Soest) und Nottuln-Uphoven (Kr. Coesfeld). Studien zum Jungneolithikum in Westfalen. Rahden: Verlag Marie Leitdorf, 320 p.

LARSSON, M.; RZEPECKI, S. 2003. Pottery, axes and houses. The earliest TRB culture in Southern Sweden and Central Poland. Lund: Lund Archaeological Rewiev (2003/2004) 8/9, p. 1-21.

LICHARDUS, J. 1991. Die Kupferzeit als historische Epoche. Versuch einer Deutung. In Lichardus, J. ed. – Die Kupferzeit als historische Epoche. Saarbrücker Beiträge zur Altertumskunde 55. Bonn: Dr. Rudolf Habelt GMBH, p.763-800.

MIDGLEY M. 1985. The Origin and Function of the Earthen Long Barrows of Northern Europe. Oxford: BAR. 330 p. (BAR International Series; 259)

MIDGLEY, M. 2005. The Monumental Cemetries of Prehistoric Europe. Stroud: Tempus, 176 p.

NOWAK, M. 2009. Drugi etap neolityzacji ziem polskich. Kraków: Instytut Archeologii Uniwersytetu Jagiellońskiego, 717 p.

RZEPECKI, S. 2004. Społeczności środkowoneolitycznej kultury pucharów lejkowatych na Kujawach. Poznań: Wydawnictwo Poznańskie, 235 p.

Rzepecki, S. 2011. The Roots of Megalithism in the TRB culture. Łódź: Instytut Archeologii Uniwersytetu Łódzkiego, Fundacja Uniwersytetu Łódzkiego, 251 p.

Rzepecki, S. 2011a. Osady i cmentarzyska kultury pucharów lejkowatych na stanowiskach Jastrzębiec 4 i Renice 5-6. Studia i materiały nad najdawniejszymi dziejami Równiny Gorzowskiej. Poznań: Wydawnictwo Poznańskie, 148 p.

Rzepecki, S. 2013. 'Invisible tombs'. From the research on funerary rituals of communities with funnel beaker. Analecta Archaeologica Ressoviensia. Rzeszów. 8, p. 49-62.

Rzepecki, S. 2014. Palimpsest, time perspectivism and megaliths. Sprawozdania Archeologiczne. Kraków. 66, p. 9-20.

Rzepecki, S. 2015. Neighbours. Thanatology of the societies in Kuyavia in the Middle Neolithic (c. 4400-3650 BC). Sprawozdania Archeologiczne. Kraków. 67 (in print).

Schade-Lindig, S. 2008. Ein Grabmonument aus mittelneolithischer Zeit? Hessen Archäologie. Wiesbaden. 2007, p. 31-34.

Sherratt, A. 1999. Instruments of conversion? The role of megaliths in the Mesolithic-neolithic transition in north-west Europe. In Beinhauer, K. W.; Cooney, G.; Guksch, Ch. E.; Kus, S., eds. – Studien zur Megalithik. The Megalithic Phenomenon. Weissbach: BeierandBeran, p. 421-432.

Sherratt, A. 1990. The Genesis of Megaliths: Monumentality, Ethnicity and Social Complexity in Neolithic North-West Europe. World Archaeology. 22, p. 147-167.

Thevenet, C. 2007. De pierre ou de bois: coffre et architecture de la sepulture 10 du monument Michelsberg de Beaurieux (Aisne, France). In Moinat, P.; Chambon, P., eds. – Les cistes de Chamblandes et la place des coffres dans les pratiques funéraires du Néolithique moyen occidental. Actes du colloque de Lausanne, 12 et 13 mai 2006. Lausanne – Paris: Cahiers d'archéologie romande. 110, p. 143-153.

Wiklak, H. 1980. Wyniki badań wykopaliskowych w obrębie grobowca 8 w Sarnowie w woj. włocławskim. Prace i Materiały Muzeum Archeologicznego i Etnograficznego w Łodzi. Łódź. 27, p. 33-83.

Wiklak, H. 1986. Podsumowanie wyników badań wykopaliskowych w obrębie grobowca 9 w Sarnowie, woj. włocławskie. Prace i Materiały Muzeum Archeologicznego i Etnograficznego w Łodzi. Łódź. 33, p. 5-21.

Wiklak, H. 1990. Z badań nad osadnictwem kultury pucharów lejkowatych w Sarnowie na Kujawach. Sprawozdania Archeologiczne. Kraków. 42: p. 109-127.

Zápotocký, M. 1986. Die Lengyel- und Trichterbecherkultur – ihr gegenseitiges Verhältnis im Lichte der Streitäxte. In Internationales Symposium über die Lengyel-Kultur, Nove Vozokany 5.-9. November 1984. Archäologisches Institut der Slowakischen Akademie der Wissenschaften in Nitra und Institut für Ur- und Frügeschichte der Universität Wien (1986). Nitra-Wien, p. 347-356.

Zápotocký, M. 1992) Streitäxte des mitteleuopäischen Äneolithikums. Acta humaniora, Band 6. VCH Verlagsgesellschaft (1992). Wienheim, 563 p.

Chapter 2

Western Europe: France

The role of enclosures in territorial organization in the Paris Basin between 4500 and 3800 BC

Claira LIETAR
UMR 8215 – Trajectoires, Maison de l'Archéologie et de l'Ethnologie,
21 allée de l'Université – 92023 Nanterre
clairaa@hotmail.fr

Abstract

In this study we seek to analyse the link between enclosures and territorial pattern in the Paris Basin between the mid- 5th millennium and the beginning of the 4th millennium BC by attempting to understand the function of these sites (a function which is not always easy to identify and which may be multiple). At the scale of the Paris Basin, various forms of territorial models can be identified within which the enclosures play a structuring role to a greater or lesser degree. While these forms of territory may be linked to systems of flint supply, their overall origin lies in the processes of regional organization.

Keywords: *Enclosures, territories, supply systems, Middle Neolithic*

Résumé

On cherche à analyser le lien entre les enceintes et la structure territoriale dans le Bassin parisien à partir du milieu du Ve millénaire jusqu'au début du IVe millénaire, en tentant de comprendre la fonction de ces sites (qui n'est pas toujours clairement identifiée et peut être multiple). Des formes variées de modèles territoriaux peuvent être reconnues à l'échelle du Bassin parisien, dans lesquelles les enceintes jouent un rôle plus ou moins structurant. Si ces formes de territoires peuvent avoir un lien avec les systèmes d'approvisionnement en ressources siliceuses, elles sont globalement issues de processus de structuration régionaux.

Mots-clés: *enceintes; territoires, systèmes d'approvisionnement, Néolithique moyen*

General perspectives

Enclosures exhibit unprecedented development in the Paris Basin from the middle of the 5th millennium BC, during the first phase of the middle Neolithic. They are partly contemporary with the first monumental funerary monuments of 'Passy' type. The phenomenon occurs in two distinct regions of the Paris Basin: the south eastern part of the Paris basin centered on the Bassée and the Yonne Valley (Dubouloz *et al.* 1991; Mordant and Simonin 1997; Delor *et al.* 1997); the western part of the basin within the Caen plain (Marcigny *et al.* 2010; Charraud 2012).

Enclosures spread throughout the Paris Basin from 4250 BC, during the second phase of the Neolithic, which is characterised by a diversification of regionalised cultural groups (Michelsberg, Northern Chassean, Noyen Group, etc.). They are contemporary with the development of flint mining around 4000 BC.

During this period, enclosure morphology becomes increasingly complex and there is a general increase in the surface enclosed areas. The question of site function remains unanswered for the vast majority of the sites. This difficulty is the result of a lack of data concerning enclosure interiors, which are too rarely excavated in their entirety. But it is also due the difficulty of interpreting the sites whose function needs to be understood in terms of the socio-cultural and symbolic system of Neolithic communities.

A habitation function is favoured for a number of enclosures, particularly those belonging to the middle Neolithic I of the Cerny 'Barbuise' culture. A defensive function, however, is rarely attributed to middle Neolithic enclosures due to the interrupted nature of their ditches (Ghesquière *et al.* 2011;

Mordant 1982; Pillot 2009). On the other hand, the symbolic nature of the enclosures is frequently highlighted and is generally based on three arguments: the specific nature of the ritual deposits (Andersen 1997, 2004, 2010; Dubouloz *et al.* 1997; Lombardo *et al.* 1984; Méniel 1987), the absence of inner structures and the complexity of site layout (Mordant 1982; Geschwinde 2009). A functional interpretation of these sites as symbolic spaces, places for communal events, is the most favoured (Andersen 1997; Geschwinde *et al.* 2009; Whittle 1996; Whittle *et al.* 2011).

In terms of a spatial approach, the enclosures form part of a site network and their role as central places makes them key elements in the organization of this network, and a fortiori in the organization of the territorial structure. Theoretical models for territorial organization within Neolithic societies have already been proposed for the Paris Basin.

Jérôme Dubouloz (1989; *et al.* 1991) has developed a socio-economic model for the organization of the Michelsberg territory in the Aisne Valley at the turn of the 5th and 4th millennia (4250-3800 BC). Based on the ranking of settlements, the model proposes a network of complementary and interdependent sites within which certain enclosures would have played a supra-local role.

The interpretive model proposed for the Yonne Valley by Jean-Pierre Delor is similar to that described by Daniel Mordant (Dubouloz *et al.* 1991) and confirmed by Lucile Pillot (2009) in the Bassée (Seine-Yonne). In the middle Neolithic I, the territory was divided into several units that include monumental burial places, habitations, small- and medium sized enclosures, cemeteries, polishing sites and a mining site. These different territorial entities indicate that the valley was shared between 'governing elites' (Delor *et al.* 1997: 392). A phenomenon similar to that observed in Bassée occurred at the end of the Cerny with the disappearance of monumental cemeteries and the multiplication of small enclosures, followed by the appearance of large enclosures in the middle Neolithic II.

Based on these theoretical models, and using a large corpus of sites for the whole Paris Basin, a multi-scale approach to territorial organization has been adopted. The goal of this study is to understand the role of the enclosures in the territorial organization of Neolithic communities, by considering the issue of their function (at the micro-regional scale) and by highlighting the different forms of territorial models (at the macro-regional scale).

Methodology for classifying enclosures

The corpus of middle Neolithic sites of the Paris Basin includes 426 sites.[1] Only sites which have been excavated (either partially or extensively) have been recorded.

A literature-based reliability index was applied to the corpus so that the analysis would only be based on a group of sites that have a same level of documentation. Certain geographic areas might be better documented than others due to better accessibility to their documentation. In all, 66% of the recorded occupation sites were selected, comprising a total of 227 occupation sites, 35 of which are enclosures.

Drawing on the theoretical models developed for the Aisne Valley, known as 'integrated models' (Dubouloz 1989; Dubouloz *et al.* 1991), and on the classification of occupation sites developed by the 'Archaedyn' project team to evaluate the level of hierarchical organization of territories (Saligny *et al.* 2008), the definition of hierarchical classes uses multivariate statistics (Factor Analysis and Ascending Hierarchical Classification). Two criteria are used in order to evaluate the degree of hierarchical organization within each territory: on the one hand, the diversity of classes represented and, on the other, the degree of differentiation between the classes, i.e. relative amplitudes (standard deviation) of the hierarchical classes.

---

[1] Database created between 2010 and 2013 in the context of my PhD thesis: 'Territoires et ressources des sociétés néolithiques du Bassin parisien: le cas du Néolithique moyen (4500-3800 BC)'. Other data has been added to this corpus (for the Eure: Riquier 2003; for Nord-Pas-de-Calais: Manceau 2008; for Lower Normandy: Charraud 2012).

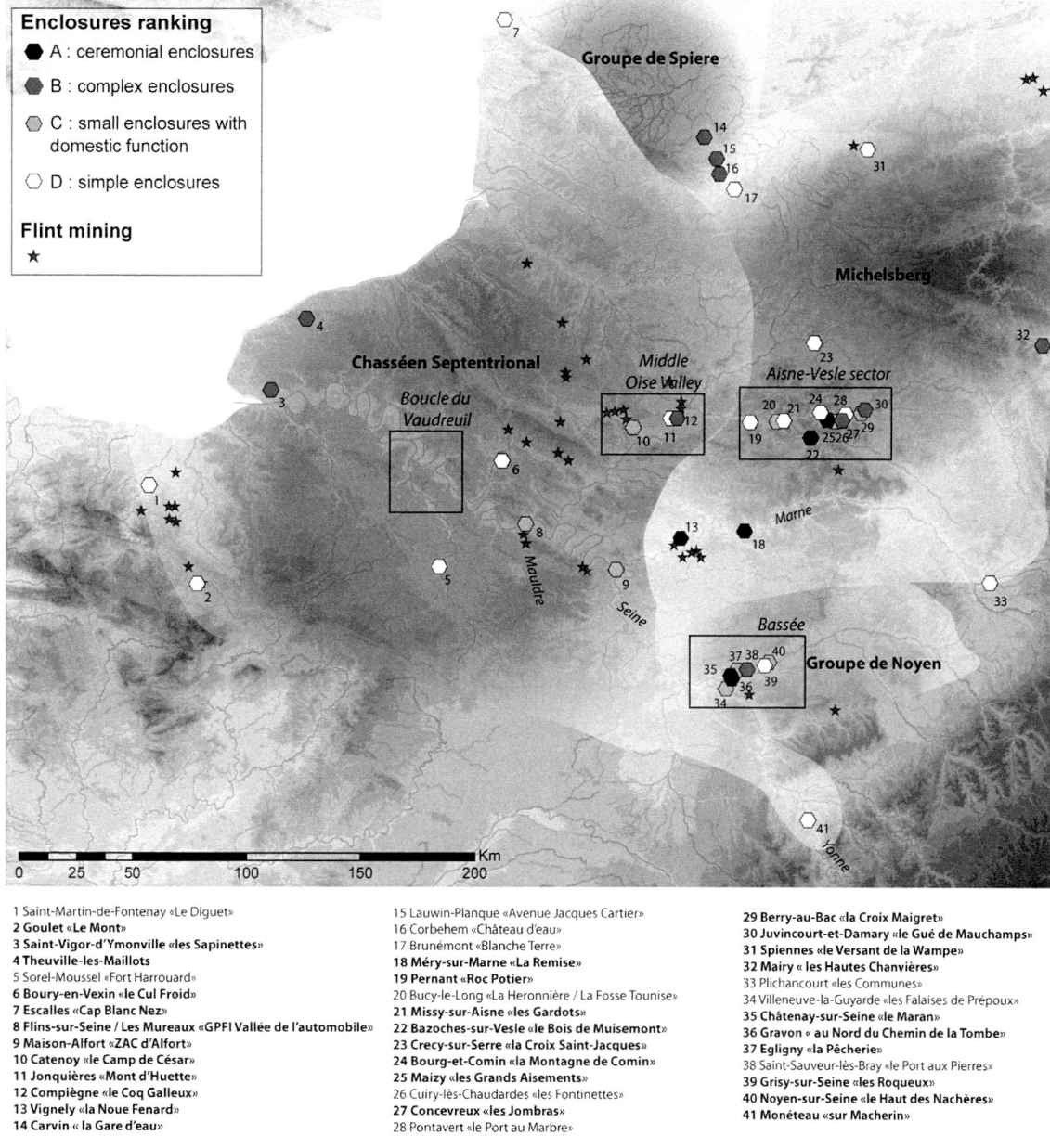

FIGURE 1. ENCLOSURES CLASSIFIED BY HIERARCHICAL RANKS FOR THE MIDDLE NEOLITHIC II (4250-3950 BC); 30 MNII ENCLOSURES USED FOR MULTIVARIATE ANALYSIS (BOLD TEXT); 11 MNII ENCLOSURES CLASSIFIED BY ANALOGY. IN THIS ARTICLE, THE ANALYSIS DOES NOT INCLUDE THE SPIERE GROUP ENCLOSURES (NOS. 14-17).

Following several tests of the criteria, the following variables were selected: enclosure dimensions (estimated total surface, overall perimeter of the structures, i.e. the cumulative total perimeter of all elements of the site); the complexity of the structures (number of ditches and/or palisades); whether or not there is evidence for a habitation function; the presence of scattered human remains and graves associated with the enclosure; and the nature of the ditch deposits.

The ascending hierarchical classification allows the corpus of 35 enclosures to be divided into four classes, known as ranks (Fig. 1):
- Rank D – Uncomplicated enclosures lacking evidence for habitation: very simple morphology (a ditch and/or a palisade), small overall perimeter (no greater than 1500 m), high degree of variation in the area enclosed which, in certain cases, can be very extensive (20 ha at

Plichancourt, 10 ha at Monéteau, 20 ha at Goulet). Rare traces of habitation are found within these enclosures. Complex deposits are rare apart from certain instances where relatively complex deposits are found which combine a variety of artefact deposits, including pottery (Crécy-sur-Serre, Goulet, Bruère-Allichamps), or notable quantities of faunal remains (Escalles, Boury-en-Vexin, Jonquières);
- Rank C – Small, simple enclosures with a habitation function: simple morphology (a ditch and palisade), small overall perimeter (less than 2500 m), small enclosed area (less than 5 ha). The habitation function may be presumed or attested;
- Rank B – Complex enclosures: simple-, complex- or very complex morphology (more than one ditch and palisade) with a large overall perimeter (greater than 1500 m). The enclosed areas vary in extent (between 4 and 15 ha, and up to 40 ha in the case of Mairy). There is evidence for a habitation function and for complex deposits (associations of artefacts, faunal deposits);
- Rank A – 'monumental' enclosures (Dubouloz et al. 1991): complex or very complex morphology (more than one ditch and palisade) and/or large overall perimeter (greater than 1300 m). The enclosed area is generally extensive (between 9 and 20 ha) but can be more restricted in certain cases (less than 4 ha for Vignely and Méry). No evidence for habitation. Relatively complex deposits (cattle skulls, faunal remains, antlers, pottery).

This classification indicates that the first phase of the Cerny 'Barbuise' enclosures, around the middle of the 5th millennium, consisted of small enclosures belonging to Rank C. During a second phase, around 4250 BC, monumental enclosures (Rank A) and complex enclosures (Rank B) developed alongside small village enclosures (Rank C). The increase in morphological complexity occurred in tandem with an increase in enclosure areas. The first examples of Rank B complex enclosures emerged during the Post-Rössen in the Aisne Valley, c. 4300 BC. Rank A enclosures, with very complex morphologies (double interrupted ditches with a palisade, or double palisades with a single ditch), are only known in Michelsberg territories from 4250 BC onwards and in the Noyen group from 4000 BC onwards. The final phase of enclosure construction, around 4000 BC, includes a high proportion of simple Rank D enclosures, particularly in Chassean territories.

In general, a diversification in the classes present and a tendency towards increasingly extensive and complex enclosures can be clearly observed. This increasing diversity suggests an evolution in terms of the function of sites which co-exist within the same territories. Using a micro-regional approach, we can attempt to throw light on site function by considering the enclosures within their environmental contexts.

The question of enclosure function: a micro-regional approach in the Aisne Valley

We have defined a micro-regional study area of 2520 km^2, centred on the Aisne and Vesle Valleys in the Department of Aisne: this was an area occupied by the Michelsberg Culture of the Paris Basin (4250-3800 BC; fig. 1).

The study area encompasses the catchment area of the Aisne, a tertiary geological context which is distinguishable from the Champagne area by virtue of its contrasting relief and numerous waterways. The valley landscape is homogenous: wet (sometimes marshy) valleys, wooded plateau slopes and edges, lutetian escarpments characterised by lower vegetation cover. The Aisne River is not very dynamic and its course has changed little since the onset of the Holocene. In general, its floodplains are the same as those of the Neolithic. The soil of the river terraces- composed of flood sediments, residual loess, sands of aeolian origin and colluvial sand-rich loams- was particularly conducive to the practice of proto-historic agriculture (Coudart and Boureux 1978). The objective of the micro-regional scale study is the modelling of environmental contexts which were conducive to the establishment of sites, in order to throw light on the relationship between the occupation sites (enclosures and other types of occupation) and their environment.

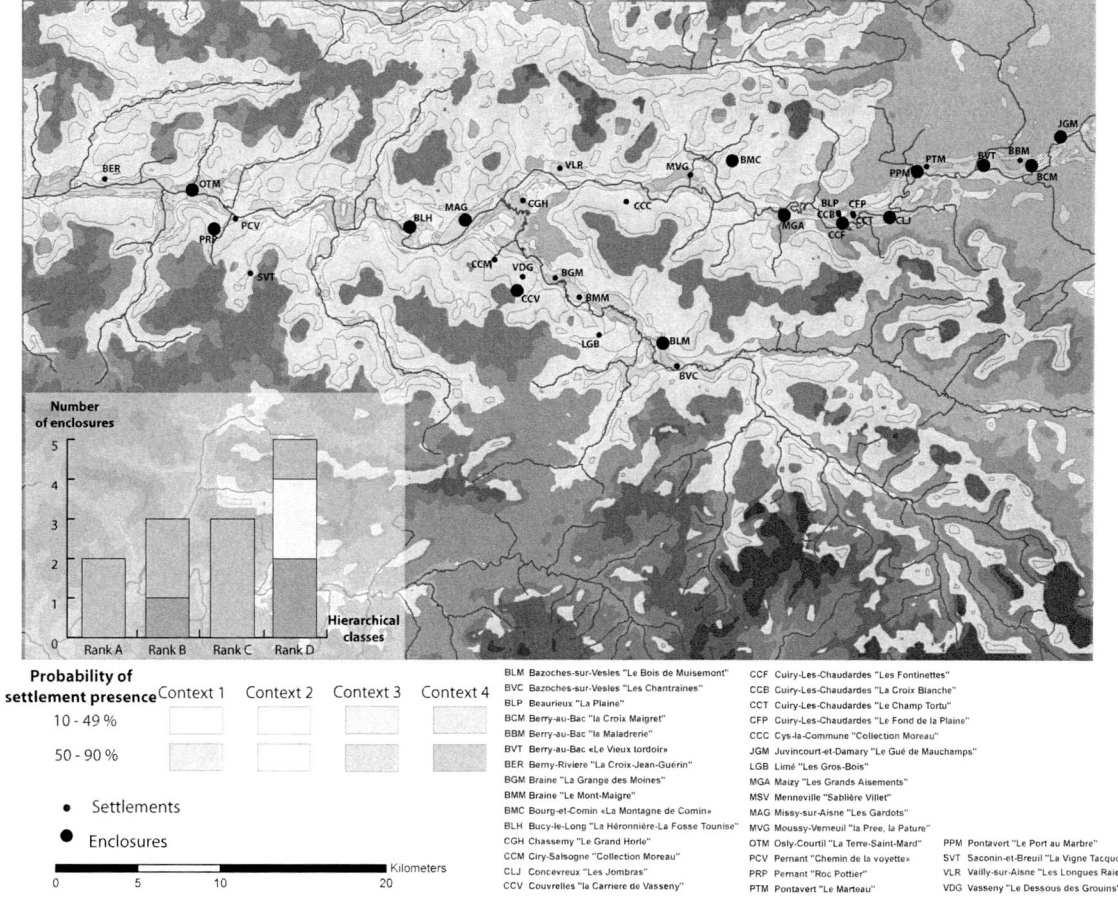

FIGURE 2. MODELLING OF ENVIRONMENTAL CONTEXTS FOR THE AISNE-VESLE SECTOR.

The term 'environmental context' refers to the proportion of environmental parameters which constitute the pixels within a circular study area around a particular site. The sites are represented by a point on the map and the radius of the study area is set at 500 m around this point. This approach permits the characterisation of the environmental context for the establishment of the site. On the basis of the site pixels, the proportion of each type of environmental variable within the study circle can be calculated.

These values are then processed using multi-variate analyses (Principal components analysis and Ascending Hierarchical Classification). The objective is to determine the environmental contexts made up of the correlated variables and the site locations.

The environmental contexts can then be modelled using the MaxEnt software program (Elith *et al.* 2011). Developed for ecological applications, the programme is used to model the distribution of species based on an estimation of the relationship between recorded data and the environmental and spatial characteristics of their location. On the basis of the Ascending Hierarchical Classification of known archaeological occupation sites, each context can be mapped by calculating the probability of the presence of sites (Fig. 2).

The variables used to reconstruct the Neolithic environment of the Aisne Valley were created for the study area and include topographical-, hydrological-, geological- and pedological data. A vectorised geological map (source: BRGM) and a vector map of the river system (source: SANDRE) were available to the project and allowed the reconstruction of the Neolithic water course.[2] Environmental variables such as distance to the watercourse and sunlight exposure (solar radiation: aerasol)[3] were produced using Arcgis with a DEM at 25 m. Finally, the landscape typology was generated by combining raster data with Spatial Analyst.

On the basis of the DEM and the geological map, maps of the natural capacity of soils to support agriculture were developed for the study area. The approach proposed here follows a pedogenetic logic without the use of classic pedological methods (field sampling, laboratory analysis, etc.). It involves defining the broad properties of soils on the basis of the geological formations described on the geological map, in combination with the topography, so as to propose a classification in terms of natural capacity for supporting agriculture.[4]

Likewise, the geological map can be reinterpreted according to hydrogeological criteria by building on the hydrogeological map. The geological formations have specific characteristics related to the permeability of the land due to the nature of the underlying materials and access to the water table (extensive, perched, deep…).

On the basis of these variables, four environmental contexts have been defined and modelled for the establishment of middle Neolithic occupation within the study area:
- Context 1 includes the wet zones located close to rivers and valley floors;
- Context 2 corresponds to the Cuisian terraces close to the perched water tables of the Laon clays and to the sparnacian clay resurgence zones;
- Context 3 corresponds to ancient, wide, alluvial terrace contexts in the vicinity of the fluvisols;
- Context 4 corresponds to ancient, wide, alluvial terrace contexts located further away from the fluvisols.

Overall, there is a general tendency for Rank A sites (monumental enclosures) and Rank C sites (small enclosures with attested evidence for habitation) to be situated in Context 3, in the transition zone between the ancient river terraces and the wet zones (Fig. 2). This is also generally the case for complex enclosures belonging to Rank B. Context 3, therefore, represents a favoured location for permanent occupation sites on the edge of the wide, flood-free terraces: it is favourable for agriculture and is also close to wet zones where the rich ecosystems provide varied vegetation and fauna and where there is access to watercourses. Monumental tombs, however, are generally situated on the flood-free terraces (context 4) beyond these transition zones.

Rank D enclosures occur in three different contexts, two of which are not contexts suited for habitation sites (Fig. 2). Some of them are found in plateau-edge contexts (Context 2). In this case the enclosures obstruct access to a spur. Where dated, the enclosures fall within the Middle Neolithic II, after 4000 BC, as is the case for the enclosures at Pernant (Le Bolloch 1981) and Bourg-et-Comin (Constantin et al. 1983).

The choice of sites dominating the valley for the enclosures highlights a new development within this territory from the latest phase of the Michelsberg (MK II and MK III; according to Dubouloz et al. 1997), between 3950 and 3800 BC. These sites could reflect a defensive function, similar to the

---

[2] In certain cases, historic variations in river meanders were revealed by commune boundaries (Boureux 1972: 117). Based on a combination of historic mapping and aerial photography, the river course outline obtained reflects the state of the Aisne in the 19th century. Because the river dynamic has been weak in the Holocene, the displacement of meanders of the Aisne is a phenomenon which only concerns the flood-prone zones situated on modern alluvial deposits (Boureux 1972).

[3] The following parameters are used to calculate sunlight values: a date of March 21st (corresponding to the Spring equinox); optimal climatic conditions (default values).

[4] The soil maps were created for two study areas: the Aisne Valley and the 'Boucle du Vaudreuil', which is located within a bend of the Seine. The process and final maps were scrutinised by two archaeologists and a geomorphologist who possess first-hand field knowledge of the area (Thierry Lepert, engineer with the Service Régional de l'archéologie de Haute-Normandie; Bruno Robert, operations manager with l'INRAP, based at Soissons; Dominique Todisco, lecturer in geography at Rouen University).

model proposed for enclosures in middle Neolithic Burgundy (Prestreau 2002). Indeed, they belong to the simplest type of enclosure (Rank D) indicating a change in purpose, and a move away from monumental sites. The finds from the partially excavated 'Roc Pottier' enclosure at Pernant include transverse arrowheads and the remains of a human leg found in the ditch (Le Bolloch 1981). These elements could be the result of conflict on the site. The enclosures on the plateau edge could also have served to manage the spaces on the valley margins in the context of agro-pastoral practices. Indeed, systems of herd management or the opening up of fields using slash-and-burn could be envisaged on the plateaux.

Other simple enclosures with small areas, such as the example at Missy-sur-Aisne (rank D), may relate to the exploitation of wet environments (Context 1) where they may, in fact, have served as livestock enclosures. However, this theory relies solely on spatial and morphological considerations: there is an absence of technical or material cultural evidence to support the hypothesis.

For each phase of the middle Neolithic, the distribution of occupation sites, including enclosures, reveals changes in the occupation of the territory. In the first phase of the Cerny period, between 4700 and 4400 BC, diverse environments are exploited with a high proportion of occupation occurring in Context 3 (the transitional zone between the alluvial terraces and the wet zones, a favoured settlement zone from the early Neolithic onwards). These occupations consist principally of habitation sites (unenclosed) or indicators of sites.

The establishment of Post-Rössen occupation sites in Context 1 (reduced or absent flood-free alluvial terraces) on the edge of the western part of the valley, an area traditionally occupied by long-term habitations since the LBK, represents a tentative expansion of an eastern-influenced cultural group between 4400 and 4200 BC. During the following Michelsberg period, this type of context is once again abandoned in favour of Context 3: an exception is to be found at Missy-sur-Aisne where a small, simple enclosure was constructed. At the end of the middle Neolithic II (3950-3800 BC) Context 2 is favoured for the construction of new enclosures that may have had a defensive function.

Just as the complementarity between sites is highly probable based on the model of territorial structuring for the Aisne Valley during the final phase of the Middle Neolithic, complementarity between the environmental contexts is also highly probable. Territorial organization can be regarded as being relatively developed during the Michelsberg Period and was based on a network of enclosures.

Comparison of territorial occupation models at a macro-regional scale

At the macro-regional scale, another sector is characterised by a high concentration and great diversity of enclosures in the Middle Neolithic II (4250-3950 BC): the Bassée situated in the Seine Valley, at the confluence with the Yonne River (Fig. 1). This broad alluvial plain, delimited by the Brie plateau to the north and the Othe region to the south, is a zone of origin and expansion for the Noyen group during the middle Neolithic II.

In the Bassée, as in the Aisne Valley, the second part of the middle Neolithic is characterised by a symbolic role for certain monumental enclosures (Rank A). They emerge in the Bassée at around 4000 BC, a little later than in the Aisne Valley: the monumental enclosure at Bazoches-sur-Vesle (in the Aisne Valley region), for example, dates from an earlier phase of the Michelsberg (MK I), between 4250 and 4050 BC (Dubouloz 1998).

However, the complexity of monumental enclosures varies between the two regions (Fig. 3). In the Bassée, the areas enclosed are very extensive while for monumental sites in the Aisne Valley, the perimeter of the enclosing elements tends to be longer, a fact which would have required greater investment in their construction (more wood required and more work involved in digging the ditches). Funerary monuments are present in the Aisne, but not in the Bassée where evidence for funerary practices is rare.

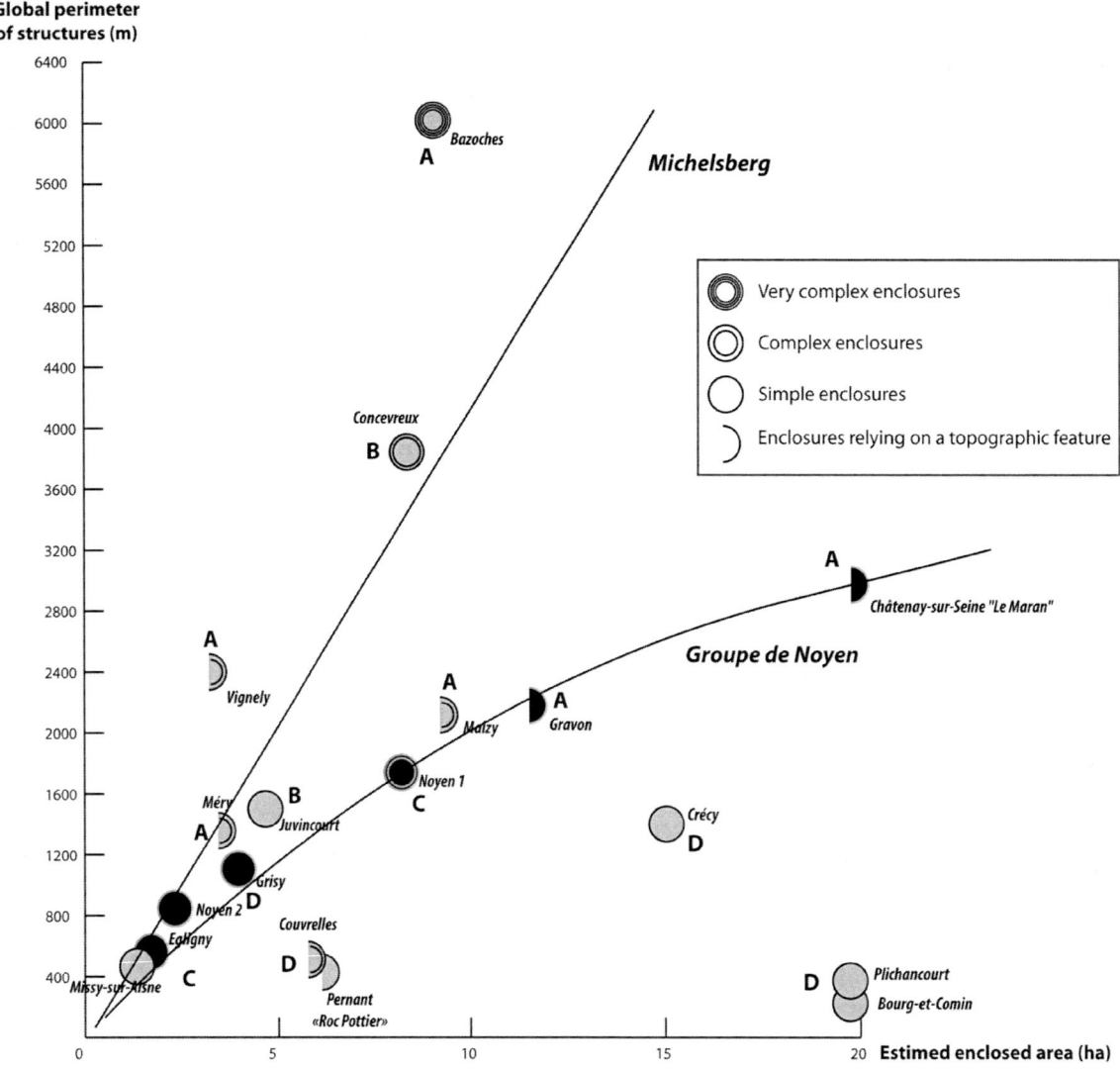

FIGURE 3. SIZE OF THE ENCLOSURES: RATIO OF THE OVERALL PERIMETER DITCHES TO THE ESTIMATED ENCLOSED AREA (MICHELSBERG ENCLOSURES IN GREY; NOYEN GROUP ENCLOSURES IN BLACK).

The diversity in hierarchical classes of occupation sites reflects a high degree of organization and gives the impression of highly structured territories in the middle Neolithic II. This approach confirms the model proposed by J. Dubouloz (1989, forthcoming) of a network of complementary, interdependent sites. Small enclosures (Rank C) reflect local socio-economic levels. Their role was primarily domestic and the investment required for the construction of the habitation and enclosing elements was relatively low compared to higher ranking enclosures. Monumental enclosures (Rank A) may depend on a regional socio-economic level. Their construction required the mobilisation of a large population. Their symbolic role, suggested by the ritual nature of several deposits, supports the hypothesis that they functioned as places of assembly for a wider community. According to this logic, Rank B enclosures, with complex structures, may have been associated with communities which were larger than those of unenclosed villages or Rank C enclosures. Rank D enclosures may have played an intermediate or marginal role on the edges of territories (on the plateaux).

Within the Chassean cultural area, however, enclosures are less numerous and more scattered (Fig. 1). The variability of enclosure classes is less than for the Michelsberg- and the Noyen Group territories. Rank A monumental enclosures are unknown in the northern Chassean culture. However, simpler enclosures (Rank D) could have hosted ceremonial activity, as evidenced by certain deposits, most notably of cattle, found in Boury-en-Vexin and in Compiègne. The presence of deposits of animal remains at this type of site is not unique to the Chassean cultural area but is a general trend during the period around 4000 BC in the Paris Basin. Such deposits have also been found in the enclosures at Escalles (Spiere Group), Vignely, Mairy (Michelsberg) and Gravon (Noyen Group).

Depending on the cultural groups, these ceremonial enclosures differ in terms of their morphology and siting. The fact that Rank A monumental enclosures, associated with the Michelsberg and Noyen Group cultures (Maizy, Vignely, Gravon, Châtenay 'le Maran'), are located close to wet zones while Rank D enclosures of the Northern Chassean (Boury-en-Vexin, Sorrel-Moussel, Jonquières) tend to occupy dominant positions, indicates cultural choices or differences in the activities carried out in the enclosures.

Middle Neolithic II territories appear to be structured to some degree around the enclosures. In some territories, occasional scattered enclosures may have acted as central places, while other territories appear to be founded on a network of enclosures with complementary functions. However, enclosures are absent in some territories within the Chassean cultural area. This is the case, for example, for the 'Boucle du Vaudreuil' area which is situated within a bend in the Seine at its confluence with the Eure (Fig. 1). It is possible to envisage different forms of territorial structuring in which enclosures play a more or less important role.

Discussion

Correlating settlement patterns and supply systems

L. Manolakakis and F. Giligny (2011) have been able to demonstrate that the scale of flint supply systems varies according to cultural groups. This raises the question of a relationship between supply systems and territorial organization.

The link between enclosures and mining has already been highlighted in the context of middle Neolithic II mining complexes which developed around 4000 BC in the Marne Valley (Lanchon *et al.* 2006; Giligny 2007; Aubry *et al.* 2014), in the Mauldre Valley (Giligny 2007), in Lower Normandy (Ghesquière *et al.* 2011) and in the middle Oise Valley (Aubry *et al.* 2014). In these territories, the enclosures were constructed in proximity to the mines and probably played a role in controlling the flint deposits.

The systems of flint supply in the territories of the Aisne Valley and the Bassée are linked to probable extraction sites situated on the valley margins, in the Romigny area in the case of the Aisne (Fig. 4), and in the Othe region for the Bassée. The territory size, consisting of the area encompassing the enclosure network and the mine or nearest flint deposit, is similar for the two valleys and covers an area roughly 40 km in diameter (Aubry *et al.* 2014).

This means of supply requires the existence of a network of distribution-, redistribution- and consumption sites, as outlined in the Spiennes model (Bostyn and Collet 2011; Aubry *et al.* 2014). According to this model, certain Michelsbeg sites in the Paris Basin, including the enclosures, could have played an important role in the redistribution of the flint raw material or flint tools. Due to its intermediate position between potential supply zones on the Tardenois Plateaux and in the Aisne Valley, the site of Bazoches-sur-Vesle, known as 'le Bois de Muisemont' (Rank A enclosure), may have played a central role in the supply of flint to Michelsberg sites (Dubouloz forthcoming; fig. 4). Similarly, the enclosure at Champigny-sur-Vesle, in the upper reaches of the Vesle Valley, may have served as a relay site for the distribution of raw flint between tertiary and secondary formation zones. This hypothesis can only be proven by excavation of the site.

In contrast to the Michelsberg and Noyen Group examples, Chassean sites were supplied with flint of local origin (i.e. from distances of 0 to 10 km) for the domestic production of flakes and axes, even

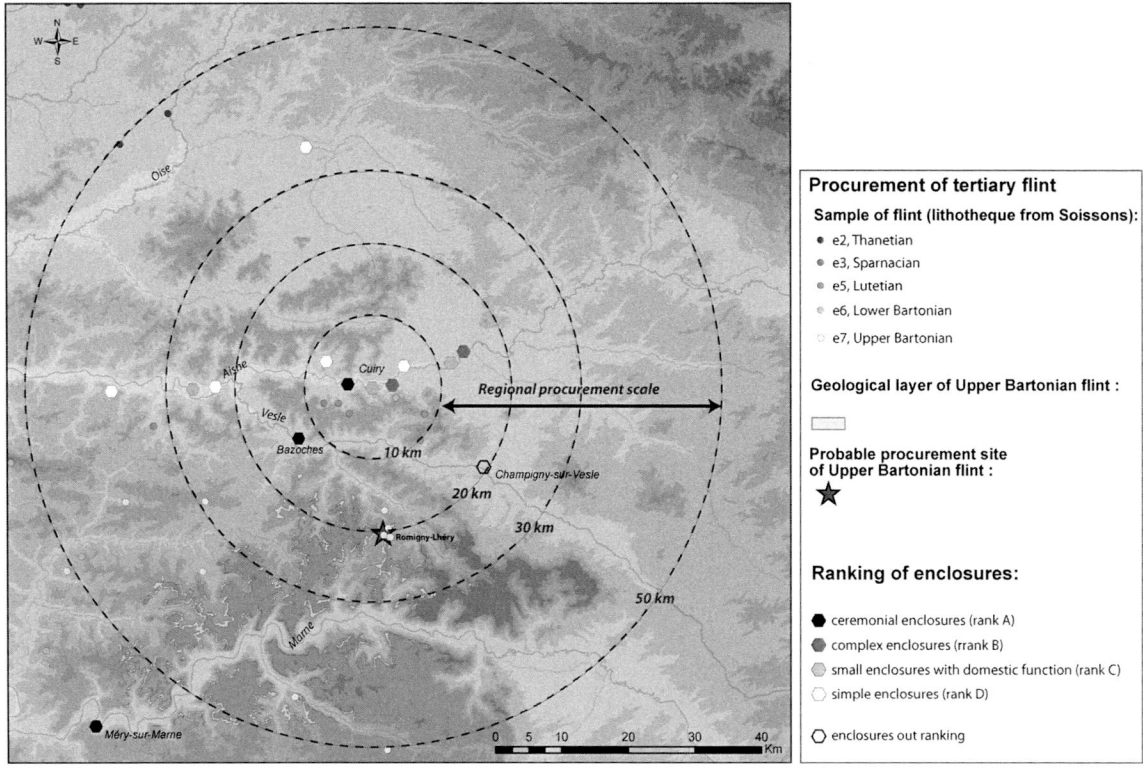

FIGURE 4. SCALES OF PROCUREMENT OF TERTIARY FLINT FROM THE PLAIN OF CUIRY-LÈS-CHAUDARDES IN THE AISNE VALLEY, MIDDLE NEOLITHIC II.

though the raw material was of only mediocre quality (Manolakakis and Giligny 2011). Furthermore, the sites are integrated within distribution networks for axes made from exogenous materials (hard rocks from the Alps or Armorican Massif) which originate from outside the region (i.e. from distances greater than 70 km). The structure of such a territory, in which the various entities are autonomous at a local scale and connected to an extra-regional economic and cultural network, is very different from the structuring evidenced in the Michelsberg territories. The 'Boucle du Vaudreuil' area, mentioned above, is typical of these territories which lack enclosures, and mining sites, and in which settlement sites benefited from local access to flint resources and also feature axes made of non-local, hard rocks.

The process of establishing territories

Several factors may explain the various forms of territorial organization. They appear to derive from regional structuring processes that are specific to each territory.

In the Aisne-Vesle and Bassée, territorial organization is strong from the middle Neolithic I onwards and is associated with the development of enclosures. Indeed, in Bassée, this structuring appears to be even older, emerging in the later Cerny (4500 BC) with an increase in the numbers of enclosures and funerary monuments in line with the model for the Yonne Valley (Dubouloz et al. 1991; Delor 1999; Duhamel and Prestreau 1997).

The diachronic approach to forms of territorial structuring in the Aisne Valley has revealed that such structuring was already highly developed in the middle Neolithic I (4500-4250 BC). In the Aisne Valley, the long sequence of occupation at certain sites (Juvincourt and Missy-sur-Aisne) and the architectural continuity evidenced by the enclosures, between the Post- Rössen period (4400-4250 BC) and the early Michelsberg (4250-3800 BC), support the hypotheses for increasing organization of site networks during these two periods, even though certain centres, such as Osly-Courtil, were clearly abandoned. The territorial organization of the middle Neolithic II was founded on the already well-structured network of enclosures of the Post-Rössen territorial model. Furthermore, it appears that the Bartonian flint diffusion networks of the Aisne Valley arose from network restructuring at the end of the early Neolithic (Prodéo *et al.* 1997). The organization of the redistribution system and the control of the resources may have contributed to the development of site networks and territorial organization from the Cerny period onwards (4700-4300 BC).

The forms of territorial occupation in the northern Chassean period appear to have been inherited from the Cerny period. Occupation consists of dispersed, unenclosed villages. Even so, the early Chassean territory of the middle Oise Valley (Fig. 1), exhibits an organization built around several enclosures from 4300/4250 BC. Its location on a major route way between the southern and northern areas of the Paris Basin, may explain the increase in the number of territorial markers in the form of enclosures in the early Chassean, around 4300 BC. This feature of territorial structuring based around enclosures has already been highlighted in the Yonne Valley (Prestreau 2002). The diffusion of axes made from Alpine rock in the south eastern part of the Paris Basin from the middle of the 5th millennium (Pétrequin *et al.* 2012), indicates the importance of such route ways and the involvement of communities in socio-economic exchange networks.

Conclusion

The increase in the numbers of enclosures in the Paris Basin in the middle Neolithic reflects the growing role played by these sites in territorial organization. This role, however, is variable.

In order to understand the phenomenon, a possible correlation between the supply system (in this case, of flint resources) and territorial organization (the role of enclosures in the supply system) could be envisaged. In the case of the Aisne Valley and the Bassée, the system of complex redistributions at a regional scale is based on a site network within which enclosures appear to play a dominant role. In contrast, an autonomous management of flint resources for domestic production allows greater independence for the habitation sites and, perhaps, a reduced role for enclosures in the organization of the supply system. However, this does not mean that complex flint supply systems systematically relied on enclosure networks, as is evidenced in the complex early Neolithic redistribution systems in the Paris Basin (Bostyn 1994; Bostyn *et al.* 2003).

Moreover, the various forms of territorial organization, regardless of whether they include enclosures or not, are linked to socio-cultural dynamics unique to each territory and are the result of local developments. Parallel to the formation of highly individualised cultural groups at the end of the 5th millennium, the regionalization of territories can be observed using specific territorial organization models.

Bibliography

ANDERSEN, N. H. 1997. The Sarup Enclosures. Moesgaard: Aarhus University Press, 404 p. (Jutland Archaeological Society Publications; XXXIII: 1).

ANDERSEN, N. H. 2004. Sarup. Causewayed enclosures placed in a Neolithic ritual landscape on Funen, Denmark. Journal of Nordic Archaeological Science. 14, p. 11-17.

ANDERSEN, N. H. 2010. Causewayed enclosures and megalithic monuments as media for shaping Neolithic identities. Journal of Neolithic Archaeology. p. 16. Available at URL: www.jungsteinSITE.de.

AUBRY, L.; BOSTYN, F.; BRUNET, V.; COLLET, H.; GILIGNY, F.; LIETAR, C.; MANOLAKAKIS, L. 2014. Territoires et ressources lithiques dans le Nord de la France et en Belgique dans l'horizon Chasséen-Michelsberg. In Louboutin, C.; Verjux, C.; Irribarria, R., eds. – Zones de production et organisation des territoires au Néolithique. Espaces exploités, occupés, parcourus. Tours: FERAC, p. 65-83 (Revue Archéologique du Centre de la France. Special number 51).

Bostyn, F. 1994. Caractérisation des productions et de la diffusion des industries du groupe néolithique du Villeneuve-Saint-Germain. Thesis. Nanterre. University of Paris 10. 2 vol.

Bostyn, F.; Giligny, F.; Lo Carmine, A.; Martial, E.; Praud, I. 2003. Production et circulation des objets en silex tertiaire bartonien dans le nord des Yvelines. In Les matières premières lithiques en préhistoire. Table-ronde d'Aurillac, 20-22 juin 2002. Préhistoire du Sud-Ouest. Suppl. n°5, p. 51-62.

Bostyn, F.; Collet, H. 2011. Diffusion du silex de Spiennes et du silex Bartonien du Bassin parisien dans le Nord de la France et en Belgique de la fin du 5e millénaire au début du 4e millénaire BC: une première approche. In Bostyn, F.; Martial, E.; Praud, I. eds. – Le Néolithique du Nord de la France dans son contexte européen: habitat et économie aux 4e et 3e millénaires avant notre ère. Actes du 29e colloque Interrégional sur le Néolithique, Villeneuve d'Ascq, octobre 2009. Revue Archéologique de Picardie. Special number 28, p. 331-348.

Boureux, M. 1972. Contribution à l'étude du Quaternaire dans le secteur tertiaire de la vallée de l'Aisne. Thèse de doctorat. Université de Paris 1.

Charraud, F. 2012. Espaces interculturels et évolution des systèmes techniques au Néolithique dans le Nord-Ouest de la France. Productions, usages et circulation des outillages en silex jurassiques de Normandie. Thesis. University of Nice Sophia-Antipolis. 2 vol.

Constantin, C.; Demoule, J.-P. 1983. Le site chalcolithique de Bourg-et-Comin ('La Montagne de Comin'). Les fouilles protohistoriques de la vallée de l'Aisne. 11, p. 137-162.

Coudart, A.; Boureux, M. 1978. Implantations des premiers paysans sédentaires dans la vallée de l'Aisne. Bulletin de la Société préhistorique française. 75: 10, p. 341-360.

Delor, J.-P. 1999. Le Néolithique de la vallée de l'Yonne (France) à travers la prospection aérienne. Revue archéologique de Picardie. Special number 17, p. 409-415.

Delor, J.-P.; Genreau, F.; Heurtaux, A.; Jacob, J.-P.; Leredde, H.; Nouvel, P.; Pellet, C. 1997. L'implantation des nécropoles monumentales, au sud du Bassin Parisien. In Constantin, C.; Mordant, D.; Simonin, D., eds. – La culture de Cerny. Nouvelle économie, nouvelle société au Néolithique. Actes du colloque international de Nemours, mai 1994. Nemours: APRAIF, p. 381-395. (Mémoires du musée de Préhistoire d'Ile-de-France. 6).

Dubouloz, J. 1989. Problématiques de recherche sur les enceintes néolithiques de la vallée de l'Aisne: un exemple représentatif du Bassin parisien? In D'Anna, A.; Gutherz, X., eds. – Enceintes, habitats ceinturés, sites perchés du Néolithique au Bronze ancien dans le sud de la France et les régions voisines. Montpellier: Mémoire de la Société Languedocienne de Préhistoire. 2, p. 55-67.

Dubouloz, J. 1998. Réflexions sur le Michelsberg ancien en Bassin Parisien. In Biel, J.; Schlichtherele, H.; Strobel, M.; Zeeb, A., eds. – Die Michelsberger Kultur und ihre Randgebiete – Probleme der Entstehung, Chronologie und des Siedlungswesens. Materialhefte zur Archäologie. Stuttgart: Band 43, Konrad Theiss V, p. 9-20.

Dubouloz, J. (forthcoming). Economic, social and political organization during the Neolithic: a multi-scale interpretation of the Middle Neolithic (4500-3800 BC) enclosures in northern France. In Gronenborn, D.; Manolakakis, L., eds. – Michelsberg culture: contributions to its misunderstanding. Mainz: Verlag des RGZ (RGZM Tagungen).

Dubouloz, J.; Hamard, D.; Le Bolloch; M. A. 1997. Composantes fonctionnelles et symboliques d'un site exceptionnel: Bazoches-sur-Vesle ('Aisne), 4000 ans av. J. C. In Espaces physiques, espaces sociaux dans l'analyse interne des sites du Néolithique à l'Age du Fer. Paris: Editions du CTHS. p. 127-144.

Dubouloz, J.; Mordant, D.; Prestreau, M. 1991. Les enceintes ' néolithiques ' du Bassin parisien. Variabilité structurelle, chronologique et culturelle. Place dans l'évolution socio-économique du Néolithique régional. Modèles interpétatifs préliminaires. In Beeching, A.; Binder, D.; Blanchet, J.-C.; Constantin, C.; Dubouloz, J.; Martinez, R.; Mordant, C.; Thevenet, C.; Vaquer, J., eds. – Identité du Chasséen. Actes du Colloque International de Nemours (1989). Nemours: APRAIF, p. 211-229. (Mémoire du Musée de Préhistoire d'Ile-de-France; 4).

Dubouloz, J.; Lanchon, Y. 1997. Cerny et Rössen en Bassin parisien. In Constantin, C.; Mordant, D.; Simonin, D., eds. – La culture de Cerny. Nouvelle économie, nouvelle société au Néolithique.

Actes du colloque international de Nemours, mai 1994. Nemours: APRAIF, p. 239-265. (Mémoires du musée de Préhistoire d'Ile-de-France; 6).

DUHAMEL, P.; PRESTREAU, M. 1997. Émergence, développement et contacts de la société Cerny en Bassin de l'Yonne. Point des connaissances et voies de recherche. In Constantin, C.; Mordant, D.; Simonin, D., eds. – La culture de Cerny. Nouvelle économie, nouvelle société au Néolithique. Actes du colloque international de Nemours, mai 1994. Nemours: APRAIF. p. 111-134. (Mémoires du musée de Préhistoire d'Ile-de-France; 6).

ELITH, J.; PHILLIPS, S. J.; HASTIE, T.; DUDÍK, M.; CHEE, Y. E.; YATES, C. J. 2011. A statistical explanation of MaxEnt for ecologists. Diversity and Distributions. 17, p. 43-57.

GESCHWINDE, M.; RAETZEL-FABIAN, D. 2009. EWBSL. Eine Fallstudie zu den jungneolithischen Erdwerken am Nordland der Mittelgebirge. Dr. Rudolf Habelt GmbH. Bonn: NRW, p. 332.

GHESQUIERE, E.; MARCIGNY, C. 2011. Construire le territoire à la fin du Ve millénaire. De grands travaux au service d'une plus grande emprise territoriale au Néolithique moyen bas-normand. Archéopages. 33. p. 6-11.

GHESQUIERE, E.; MARCIGNY, C.; AUBRY, B.; CLEMENT-SAULEAU, S.; DIETSCH-SELLAMI, M.-F.; DELOZE, V.; HAMON, G.; QUERRE, G.; RENAULT, V. 2003. L'habitat néolithique moyen I de Vivoin 'le Parc' (Sarthe). Bulletin de la Société préhistorique française. 100: 3, p. 533-573.

GILIGNY, F. 2007. Systèmes techniques et territoires dans la vallée de la Seine et le Bassin parisien au Néolithique. 'Thèse d'habilation à diriger des recherches'. University of Paris 1. 2 vol.

LANCHON, Y.; BRUNET, P.; BRUNET, V.; CHAMBON, P. 2006. Fouille de sauvetage d'un monument funéraire et d'une enceinte néolithiques à Vignely 'la Noue Fénard' (Seine-et-Marne). Dijon: Revue Archéologique de l'Est. Suppl. 25, p. 335-351.

LE BOLLOCH, M. 1981. Le site chalcolithique de Pernant ('Le Roc Pottier'). Les fouilles protohistoriques de la vallée de l'Aisne. 9, p. 161-170.

LOMBARDO, J. L.; MARTINEZ, R.; VERRET, D. 1984. Le site chasséen du Culfroid, à Boury-en-Vexin dans son contexte historique et les apports de la stratigraphie de son fossé. Amiens: Revue archéologique de Picardie. 1-2, p. 269-283.

MANCEAU, L. 2008. Le Néolithique du Nord-Pas-de-Calais: synthèse documentaire et approche spatiale. Mémoire de Master 1. Université Paris I. 2 vol.

MANOLAKAKIS, L.; GILIGNY, F. 2011. Territories and lithic resources in the Paris Basin during the Middle Neolithic (4200-3600 BC). In Capote, M.; Consegrua, S.; Diaz-Del-Rio, P.; Terradas, X.; eds. – Proceedings of the 2nd International Conference of UISPP Commission on Flint Mining Pre- and Protohistoric Times. Oxford: B.A.R. p. 45-50 (BAR international Series; 2260).

MARCIGNY, C.; GHESQUIERE, E.; JUHEL, L.; CHARRAUD, F. 2010. Entre Néolithique ancien et Néolithique moyen en Normandie et dans les îles Anglo-Normandes. Parcours chronologique. In Billard, C.; Legris, M., eds. – Premiers Néolithiques de l'Ouest. Cultures, réseaux, échanges des premières sociétés néolithiques à leur expansion, Colloque interrégional sur la Néolithique, Le Havre, 9-10 novembre 2007. Rennes: PUR, p. 117-162.

MÉNIEL, P. 1987. Les dépôts d'animaux du fossé chasséen de Boury-en-Vexin (Oise). Revue archéologique de Picardie. 1: 1-2. p. 3-19.

MORDANT, C. 1982) – Le Néolithique moyen récent dans le bassin de l'Yonne, in Le Néolithique de l'Est de la France, Actes du Colloque Néolithique, Sens, 1980. Société archéologique de Sens. Cahier n°1. p. 171-176.

MORDANT, C.; POITOUT, B. 1982. Le Néolithique moyen récent dans le bassin de l'Yonne. Société archéologique de Sens. Cahier n°1, p. 171-176.

MORDANT, D.; SIMONIN, D. 1997. Sites d'habitat Cerny. In Constantin, C.; Mordant, D.; Simonin, D., eds. – La culture de Cerny. Nouvelle économie, nouvelle société au Néolithique. Actes du colloque international de Nemours, mai 1994. Nemours: APRAIF, p. 319-339. (Mémoires du musée de Préhistoire d'Ile-de-France; 6).

PETREQUIN, P.; CASSEN, S.; GAUTHIER, E.; KLASSEN, L.; PAILLER, Y.; SHERIDAN, A. with the collaboration of DESMEULLES, J.; GILLIOZ, P.-A.; LE MAUX, N.; MILLEVILLE, A.; PÉTREQUIN, A.-M.; PRODÉO, F.; SAMZUN, A.; FABREGAS VALCARCE, R. 2012. Typologie, chronologie et répartition des grandes haches alpines en Europe occidentale. In Petrequin, P.; Cassen, S.; Errera, M.; Klassen, L.;

Sheridan, A.; Petrequin, A.-M., eds. – Jade. Inégalités sociales et espace européen au Néolithique: la circulation des grandes haches en jades alpins. Besançon: Presses Universitaires de Franche-Comté, p. 574-727 (Cahiers de la MSHE Ledoux).

Pillot, L. 2009. L'Occupation du sol au Néolithique dans la vallée de la Seine et la zone de confluence Seine-Yonne: analyses statistiques et spatiales des types d'occupation. Mémoire de Master 2 Professionnel Archéosciences et Géo Environnement. Université de Bourgogne. 161 p.

Prestreau, M. 2002. Enceintes néolithiques de Bourgogne: bilan et axes de recherches. Dijon: Revue Archéologique de l'Est. 51, p. 429-449.

Prodeo, F.; Constantin, C.; Martinez, R.; Toupet, C. 1997. La culture de Cerny dans la région Aisne-Oise. In Constantin, C.; Mordant, D.; Simonin, D., eds. – La culture de Cerny. Nouvelle économie, nouvelle société au Néolithique. Actes du colloque international de Nemours, mai 1994. Nemours: APRAIF, p. 169-186. (Mémoires du musée de Préhistoire d'Île-de-France; 6).

Riquier C. 2003. Caractéristiques de l'implantation du Néolithique dans le département de l'Eure (27). Application d'un système d'information géographique. Mémoire de DEA de l'Université de Paris 1. 42 p.

Saligny, L.; Nuninger, L.; Ostir, K.; Poirier, N.; Fovet, E.; Gandini, C.; Gauthier, E.; Kokalj, Z.; Tole, F., with the collaboration of the ArchaeDyn team 2008. Models and tools for territorial dynamic studies. In 7 millennia of territorial dynamics settlement pattern, production and trades from Neolithic to Middle Ages. Colloque ArchæDyn – Dijon, 23-25 june 2008. Dijon: ARCHÆDYN (Preprints), p. 25-44.

Whittle, A. 1996. Europe in the Neolithic: The Creation of New Worlds. Cambridge: C.U.P., 460 p.

Whittle, A.; Healy, F.; Bayliss, A. 2011. Gathering Time. Dating the Early Neolithic Enclosures of Southern Britain and Ireland. Oxford: Oxford Books. vol. 1, 992 p.

Late Neolithic graves and enclosures in Lower Languedoc: A phenomenon of alternation, 3200-2200 cal. BC

Luc JALLOT
Université Paul Valéry-Montpellier, UMR 5140 'Archéologie des Sociétés, Médierranéennes', Labex Archimède: 'Archéologie et Histoire de la Méditerranée et de l'Égypte anciennes'
ljallot@9business.fr

Abstract

The late Neolithic of eastern Languedoc (South-east France) is exemplified by the Ferrières (3200-2600 cal. BC) and Fontbouisse (2600-2200 cal. BC) cultures. Innitially, parallel to passage graves (dolmens) sometimes grouped in necropoli, numerous karstic cavities served as graves. Little is visible of the habitation site. Subsequently chambered tombs were no longer built. Open villages and enclosures, sometimes of considerable amplitude, cover the whole territory. Graves and necropolis on one side, villages and enclosures on the other side, share the communal space according to a phenomenon of alternation which permits us to propose an explication of historical and social order.

Keywords: *Enclosures, graves, late Neolithic, cultural transition*

Résumé

Le Néolithique final du Languedoc oriental (Sud-Est de la France) est illustré par les cultures de Ferrières (3200-2600 av. J.-C.) et de Fontbouisse (2600-2200 av. J.-C.). Dans un premier temps de nombreuses cavités karstiques servent de tombes, parallèlement aux dolmens à couloir parfois groupés en nécropoles. L'habitat est peu visible. Par la suite, les dolmens ne sont plus construits. Les villages ouverts et des enceintes d'ampleur parfois importante couvrent tout le territoire. Tombes et nécropoles d'une part, villages et enceintes d'autre part, participent de l'espace communautaire selon un phénomène d'alternance qui permet de proposer une explication d'ordre historique et social.

Mots-clés: *Enceintes, tombes, Néolithique final, transition culturelle*

Introduction

In south-eastern France, a long mastery of building techniques gave the small communities of the Fontbouisse culture (2600-2200 cal. BC) the means to increase the amplitude of their architectural realizations. This no longer concerns the deceased who only rarely impose the edification of an ostentatious monument but implicates the habitation. Then there is the question of the identification of new funerary places and their relationship with stone enclosures.

Environmental conditions play an significant role in this scheme. The eastern part of Languedoc also called lower Languedoc is divided into three main units. Bordering on the coast, one distinguishes a littoral plain bordered by a chain of lagoons and lakes, crossed by tresses of little coastal rivers. In the hinterland, a karstic type of landscape opens up, composed of low hills and plateau, and an exposed limestone substratum with enclaves of sedimentary basins. The whole is dominated by a third level, stretching from the north of the Cevennes, to the north-west by the high plateaux of the Grands Causses and the Montagne Noire.

The end of the Neolithic is divided into five phases. The first or late Neolithic 1 (3400-3200 cal. BC) is characterized by a sparsely decorated pottery inherited from the middle Neolithic and the collectivization of tombs (Gutherz and Jallot 1995). If the first enclosed spaces appear at the end of that period, the habitation is badly characterized and dispersed. The tombs are more like collective ossuaries in caves and are still little known in the plain where they are represented by possibly individual tombs, under mound (Hasler *et al.* 1998). The late Neolithic 2, is essentially represented by the Ferrieres group (3200-2800 cal. BC). The pottery is decorated with incised lines, impressions and *pastillages* on non-segmented forms. The funerary sites are very numerous and amount to at last 2000 occurrences for lower Languedoc alone (Gutherz *et al.* 2010). They yield a diversified ornamentation in rock, shell and bone; one notes the presence of some metallic objects (beads in copper, often native).The lithic industry is varied with the utilization of flint as tablets extracted from mines. The art is characterized by the first anthropomorphic steles. A terminal phase of this culture, so-called 2 B or Epiferrieres (2900/2800-2600 cal. BC), saw the development of an autochthonous copper metallurgy (Guilaine 1997; Ambert 2006) and a poorly decorated ceramic (Jallot 2003). It is at this period that the large enclosures of the Aude valley appear and that one notes an early densification of the habitation site. The transition to the Fontbouisse culture, around 2600 cal. BC, is accompanied by a considerable densification of the population until the disappearance of that culture towards an horizon of 2200/2100 cal. BC, from 2400 cal. BC. Its development is parallel with the Beaker culture (Lemercier 2004). The Fontbouisse culture is characterized by the production of a fine, richly decorated, ceramic with a carinated profile, by diversified ornaments and an abundant production of objects in copper. In the hinterland, some stone enclosures were built in concurrence with numerous open villages. The plains and coastal valleys become covered with vast settlements showing networks of ditches. Anthropomorphic steles are still produced. The diversity of funerary practices, collective and sometimes individual is notable. The transition to the early Bronze Age (a possible fourth phase around 2150 cal. BC) still poses many unsolved questions. The role of the Beaker culture and of the Neolithic substratum has still not been completely elucidated (Jallot 2010).

1. The late Neolithic 2 and the Ferrieres culture: first enclosures and necropolis

1.1. Habitation site

The habitation sites of the Ferrieres culture are generally small, isolated settlements formed by a grouping of five to ten ditches. Pending more significant discoveries, it concerns a dispersed habitation site corresponding to small groups of possibly itinerant farmers (Jallot 2011). During the Late Neolithic 2B, around 2800 cal. BC, we observe the formation of more extensive, partly homogenous settlements, as at La Plaine de Chretien or at La Cavalade (Montpellier, Hérault). An original model of a cellar, occasionally faced, probably served to conserve perishable provisions contained in vessels or baskets secured in little cavities (Jallot 2014). A small village of metalworkers at La Capitelle du Broum (Peret, Hérault) with houses in stone is established In the proximity of copper mines (Ambert *et al.* 2002). On the site of Les Vautes (St Gely-du-Fesc, Hérault) a house also built in dry-stone yielded a well preserved archaeological floor.

These hamlets comprising some buildings with rounded facade prelude the houses of phase 3. In face of these constructions which one could qualify as an open village a new phenomenon emerges, hill top sites surrounded by an enclosure or defended by a moat or a rampart. Enclosures and spurs barred with a fosse are established from one end of the Hérault valley to another. A fosse closes a spur at Roquemengarde (St Pons-de-Mauchiens, Hérault), also at Puech Badieu (Mèze, Hérault). At Puech Haut (Paulhan, Hérault), on a hill dominating the Hérault plain, a small quadrangular building of wooden posts is surrounded by a light palisade (Carozza *et al.* 2005). A similar phenomenon appears at the same epoch in western Provence and in the valley of the Aude (Jallot 2010, *op. cit.*).

1.2. Tombs

Some centuries after the disappearance of the giant monuments of Western France, megalithic coffers are common throughout Mediterranean Languedoc. A long trail of megalithic sepultures amount to over three thousand 'dolmens'. If Chassean coffers, called pre-megalithic, are known, the chambered and antechambered tombs of eastern Languedoc are contemporary to the Ferrieres pottery style. They can form a necropolis from five to twenty monuments. Yet, these groups are exceptional, isolated monuments are the rule and they are generally never associated with traces of a habitation site. Collective sepultures qualified as hypogea, disposed in artificial cavities are attested from the late Neolithic 2 as at Serre de Bernon (Laudun, Gard). At Cadereau d'Alès (Nîmes, Gard), a vast circular excavation provided with a sort of ramp hollowed out at its base with several alcoves containing individual inhumations (Gutherz *et al.* 2010, *op.cit.*). At La Cavalade (Montpellier), in the vicinity of the habitation site a large pit contains a complex collective burial formed by the heaping up of several hundreds of bodies (Unpublished work). But, individual deposits in a cave or crevice are also known. Multiple deposits are rarely isolated. Again at La Cavalade, multiple burials were brought to light in pits, in the very midst of the habitation site. And yet it's difficult to speak of a necropolis, that notion suggesting the gathering together of several funerary monuments or of isolated tombs.

1.3. General view

In the rocky hinterland, houses are built with stones walls. In the coastal valleys, on loamy soil, pits are dug probably associated with buildings of wood or daub whose trace has not been conserved. The possible links between these necropolis and the habitation sites and a fortiori with the few Late Neolithic 2B enclosures pointed out in the Hérault valley area, cannot be established. However, it should be underlined that the regions where a system of delimitation is found: on the one hand the Aude and Hérault valleys and on the other hand western Provence, encircle lower Languedoc with its great concentration of chambered tombs (dolmens). Despite everything, one cannot conclude a strict opposition between the two types of monumental architecture, to the extent that the phenomenon of enclosures in Aude accompanies the construction of great passage graves. Similarly, in Provence, the earliest hill top habitation sites with a barrage wall are contemporary with necropolis of hypogea at Cordes, near Arles, which count among the most imposing funerary monuments of Western Europe (Laporte *et al.* 2011). One should rather envisage different situations in a strongly contrasted cultural landscape. This phase already takes into account the opposition between the hinterlands and the coast, which will assert itself in the following period (Gutherz and Jallot 1999).

2. The late Neolithic 3 and the culture of Fontbouisse: partitions and exclusions

2.1. The habitation site of the hinterland: open hamlets and enclosures

During the second half of the third millennium, the hinterlands of Nimes and Montpellier present an exceptional concentration of prehistoric hamlets (Gutherz 1975; Gasco 1976). Houses built in dry-stone certainly represent the oldest habitations still in partial elevation in our country (Fig. 1A). The village of Cambous is the best studied (Canet and Roudil 1978). The hamlets are sometimes surrounded by small circular constructions of about five meters in diameter (Gutherz and Jallot 1989). Lébous excavated in the sixties by Jean Arnal is the habitation site of reference (Fig. 2A). Its very particular characteristics led the prehistorian to assimilate it to a fortified village, protected by towers after the 'castros' of Portugal (Arnal 1973). Other enclosures in the polygonal style have been identified by fieldwalking. Their number does not exceed fifteen, which represents about ten percent of the Fontbouisse settlements in the hinterlands of Montpellier and Nimes.

The excavations at Boussargues have shown that the Lébous 'towers' are simply sorts of storerooms or shed originally corbelled like the modern 'bories' of Provence and 'capitelles' of Languedoc (Colomer *et al.* 1990). However, a defensive function is not excluded. Nevertheless, so many 'towers' are not to be confirmed absolutely indispensable for defense against an attack of this small enclosure. As in other enclosures, the site has not yielded metalworking material, as in the case of other enclosures. The spacing between the circular structures (between 26 m and 33 m) are below the firing range of a sling dangerous as far as 40-60 m. Boussargues is more of a specialized habitation site. The inhabitants were devoted to the gathering of holm oak acorns and their transformation into flour just before the burning of their village. Observation permits to propose the hypothesis of a co-habitation of two distinct groups, no doubt, familial, who came together at the occasion of this seasonal activity (Jallot 1990). Each family possesses a set of vases, grinding implements, and cooks

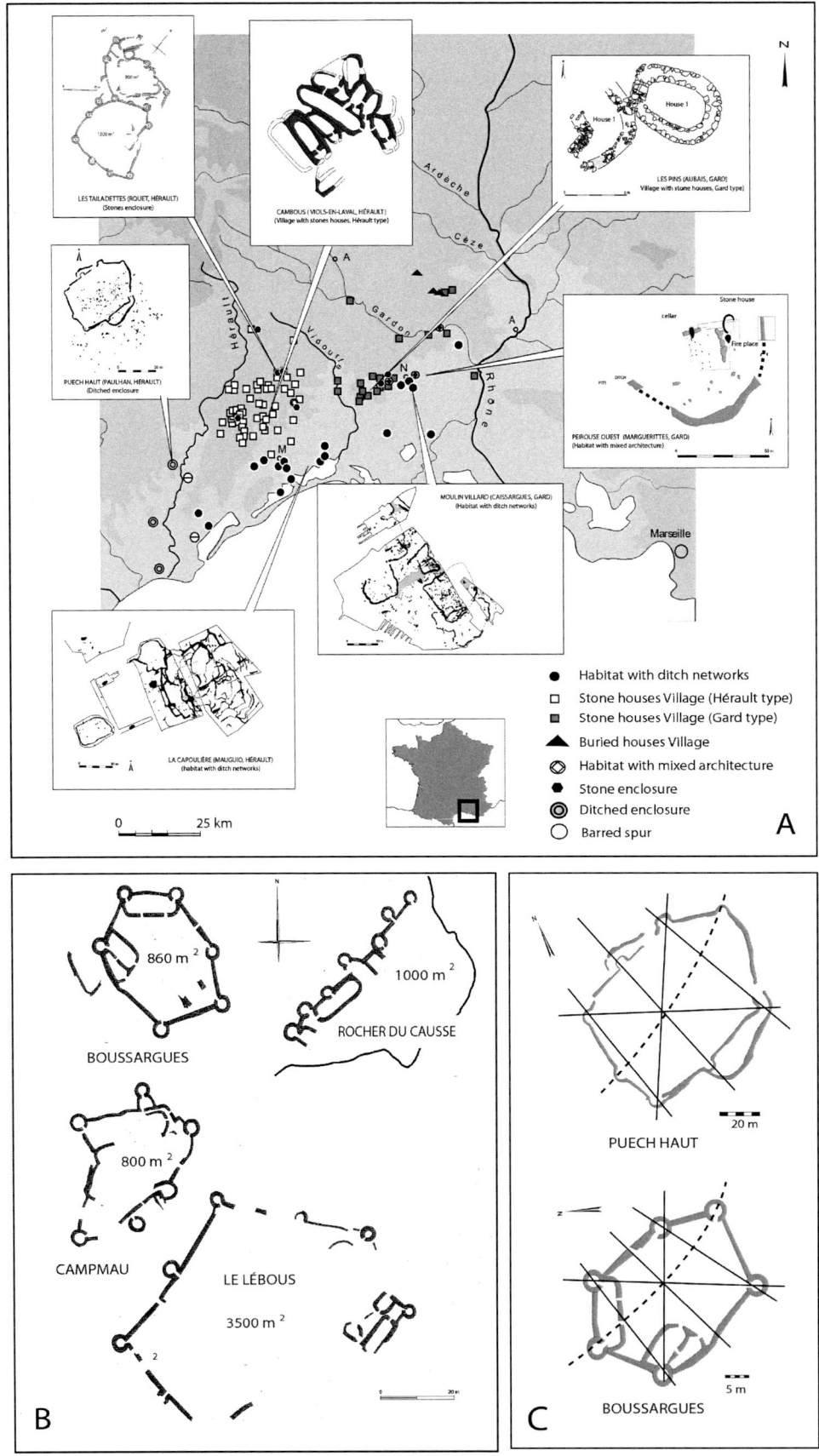

Figure 1. A: styles of habitats in the Fontbouisse culture (2600-2200 cal. BC); B: polygonal enclosures and bared spurs of the Fontbouisse culture; C: comparison between sites of Boussargues and Puech Haut which show a similar organization of their plan (B: composed with Coularou *et al.* 2008; C: composed with Carozza *et al.* 2005 and author).

their own food. Two assortments of vases arranged around the hearths are equivalent in number and in volume.

These two sets of kitchen utensils are distinguished from each other by the form and ornamentation of the receptacles (Fig. 2A). The setting up of round structures guides the architectural project. Two possible axes determine the development of the enclosure.'s polygon. Other correspondences of symmetry have been identified on habitation sites whose architectural features come close to Boussargues: le Rocher du Causse (Claret, Hérault) and to Vignaud 3 (Langlade, Gard); a similar observation holds for le Puech Haut enclosure (Paulhan, Hérault). These correspondences of symmetry cannot be due to chance or to topography alone, they are the consequence of planning. A re-examination of the data permits the underlining of the great homogeneity of these stone enclosures and confirms Boussargues' status as a seasonal habitation site. Its general plan and its chronology implicitly points to the large semicircular enclosure with bastions of le Puech Haut whose construction also seems to date to the end of late Neolithic 3 (Fig. 1C).

2.2. Return to the Iberian enclosures?

The perception of Fontbuxian enclosures, notably that of Lebous, has been much influenced by the monumental character of the Portuguese 'castros'. One saw in their edification the direct influence of eastern settlers, of a 'Beaker people'. These theories are no longer held (Cardoso 1997), but comparisons of the general organization of plans (walls linking the 'towers') has led to recognizing the influence of a cultural current issuing from Portugal and southern Spain. Nevertheless, the width of the Languedocian enclosure walls and their development has nothing in common with the Iberian realizations. Besides their number and the originality of their architecture, the interest of the Iberian enclosures is also to be found in the empty bastions of very similar conception, in semi-circle, oval or subquadrangular plan. The deep meaning of the bastions is no doubt to be sought in the global expression of territorial anchorage of small agro-pastoral communities relating to a form of economic success. One can supposes a convergence of intention at the origin of a convergence of plan, but this explication does not appear to be sufficient. In fact, surrounding a habitation site with a protection, wall or bank, is not exceptional in itself, but to build circular cells against it points to a common incentive, perhaps a concept which elsewhere is not generalized, because only certain regions of southern Europe present this combination of enclosure wall and bastions or circular structure, a combination which will only be widely adopted during the Proto-historic period. Furthermore, it is from the image of Iron age fortifications that are forged archaeological notions of Neolithic entrenchments. However, the circular structures and the bastions of le Puech Haut are different from the Iberian arrangements. In most cases, the latter are contiguous and not inclusive structures. Nevertheless, he question of the influence of the model of the Iberian bastion still remains. The link with the Beaker culture is hardly evident since the witnesses of that culture correspond to the last phases of occupation of the Languedocian enclosures, when the ditches are almost choked up and the walls have collapsed. The bell beaker silhouette is an expressive form understood by distant populations, like the 'T' faces of the anthropomorphic stelae, the ornaments of rare stones, certain types of arms; the enclosure with circular structures is perhaps another? To admit the globality of the phenomenon of enclosures with contiguous cells during the IIIrd millennium from the Atlantic to the Mediterranean West implicitly leads to admit a general movement of diffusion of a cultural norm through a very vast region. On the other hand, its diffusion from place to place is easier to explain, if one prefers to see in this combination a model adopted through imitation to signify a fact understandable for everyone.

2.3. The habitation site of the plains and alluvial valleys: ditched enclosures

The habitation sites of the plains and alluvial valleys are also qualified as enclosures. However, they present very different plans and spatial organization. Extended settlements cover surfaces from 5 to 20 ha (Jallot 2011 *op. cit.*). They present a network of sinuous ditches surrounding groups of pits (Fig. 1A). These coalescent enclosures from 2 to 3000 m², of rectangular or oval plans, constitute the

Giants in the Landscape: monumentality and territories in the European Neolithic

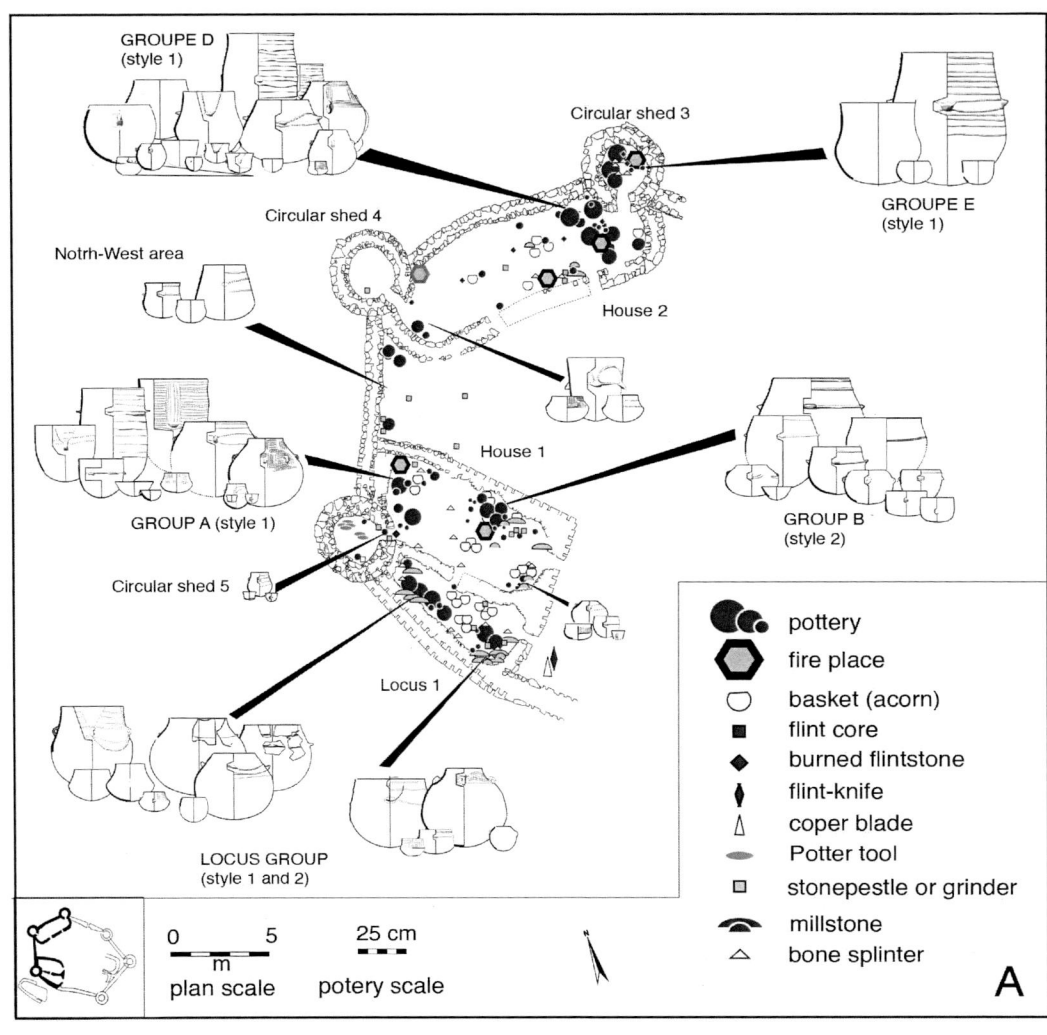

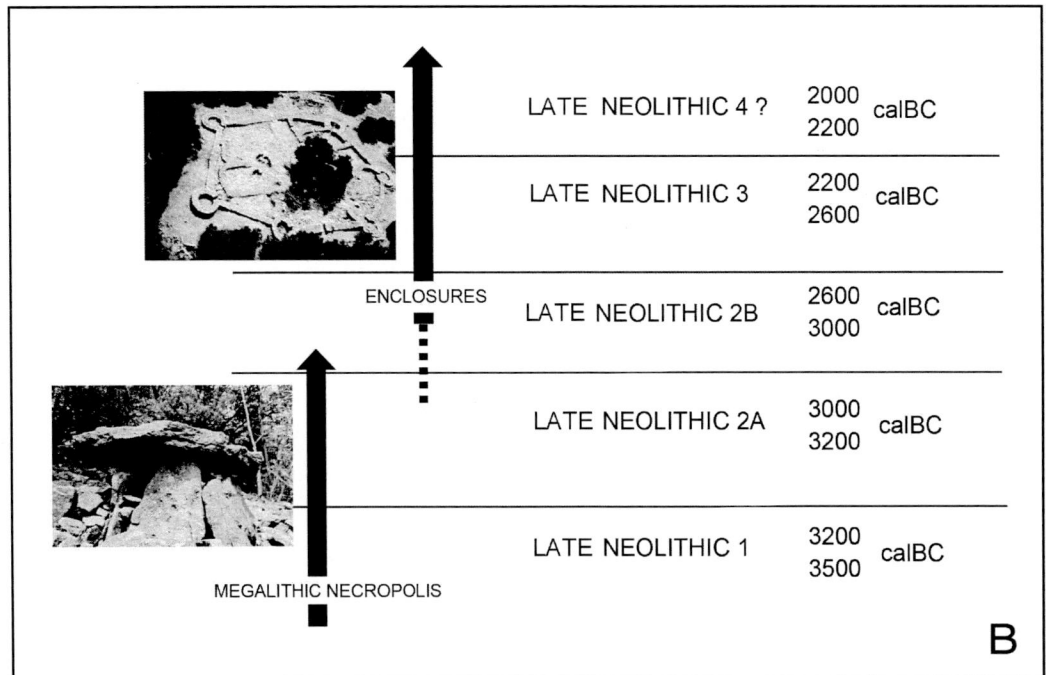

Figure 2. A: the enclosure of Boussargues: domestic activities are attested by organization of items in the domestic area. B: the oscillating movement between megalithic necropolis and enclosures expresses all the more the growing importance of land and the extension of settlement limits in view of the socialization of the landscape of Fonbouisse culture.

heart of the site. Their periphery is occupied by other enclosures, quarries for sediments or pits for ensilage. Certain ditches remain open, others maintain a palisade. However, some earth-works have a monumental character, such as the wide and deep ditch doubled by a palisade bordering the habitation site of the Stade Richter (Montpellier) or the stone faced ditch of west Peirouse (Margueritttes).

In the Hérault valley, le Puech Haut continues to be occupied and enclosures multiply in the Beziers area. These sites are villages. The enclosures, provided with wide access and whose fillings yield traces of dung, are manifestly reserved for cattle. The concentration of pits converted into middens and the abundance of domestic refuse indicates the inhabited zones (Carozza *et al.* 2005, *op. cit.*). The volume of earth extracted at the time of digging probably served for the raising of banks along the ditches. Their traces are sometimes found in the fillings. But this earth once sieved could serve in the construction of habitations in daub. Relatively well-preserved walls are built in this manner on the site of la Capoulière 2 (Mauguio, Hérault) (Gutherz *et al.* 2011, *op. cit.*). The remains' state of preservation does not permit to grasp the village's complete plan, but various indications make it possible to suppose the establishment of small houses along the ditches. Fragments of plaster come from the inner walls and modeled surfaces show the presence of decoration on the façades. At Mas de Vignoles IV (Nîmes) the ditches are filled with layers of debris of constructions in unfired clay. It is quite possible that this settlement towards the end of its occupation was a part of a small terraced tell whose imprint no doubt marked the landscape for a long time after its disaffection (Jallot 2004).

Certain ditches are made up of the alignment of independently dug pits, which are set-off at their extremities. Their length could correspond to the space cleared by the work of one person. Construction by module is envisaged for Los Millares site whose enclosure wall is built in successive sections. This process is attested for the Fontbuxian villages of Gard and of Hérault. The architectural complexity of certain collective realizations could result entirely from the investment of several groups of builders and be inscribed after a symbolic manner in the construction's segmentation (Diaz-Del-Rio 2008).

2.4. The tombs

In the hinterland, the sepulchral caves continue to be favoured by the inhabitants. Ancient chambered tombs (dolmens) are reinvested or transformed. Coffers under mound or small oval constructions delimited by stone walls called 'oval tombs' contain collective burials. In the villages of the limestone hinterland the dead are deposited in pot-holes, rearranged ruins or as at Cambous in jars placed in habitations. On the habitation site of Terruge (Collias, Gard), a tiny shelter under a bank of tufa, in contact with the domestic areas, contains two skeletons buried in the midst of a crown of blocks and querns. The late Neolithic funerary groups brought to light in the plains and alluvial valleys of eastern Languedoc between the end of the eighties and the beginning of the years two thousand remain largely unpublished. These groups generally placed in the heart of the habitation sites, are mainly individual tombs in pits. Double or multiple tombs are infrequent and one takes into account some secondary deposits. The elaborated architectures are still exceptional and correspond to the faced pits sometimes associated with a tumulary mass, as in the case of the mound at west Peirouse (Margueritttes, Gard). In the plain collective burials of the 'oval tomb' type are found as well as individual burials in a pit. At la Capouliere (Mauguio, Hérault) and at Moulin Villard (Caissargues, Gard) the disposition of sepulchral pits containing one single inhumation follows privileged alignments. However, in the absence of absolute dating, it is not certain if all these groups are of the late Neolithic. If a possible organization of the funerary space can be put into relation with the space of the living, it remains to demonstrate the coexistence or the superposition of one and the other.

2.5. General view

The enclosed villages of the hinterland present an astonishing homogeneity above all expressed through the standard of dry-stone circular structures. The study of the site of Boussargues confirms its use as a seasonal habitation site engaged in a specialized production. The enclosure's edification refers to a pre-established and segmentary model, ordered by the construction of circular structures. In another register, the unity of the plans of Boussargues and of le Puech Haut illustrates a common architectural conception. Their dating in the last third of the third millennium reinforces this link, but should be confirmed. Even if this affinity constitutes a particular case, it shows the primacy of an architectural standard which surpasses cultural discontinuities. Sites with round structures or bastions should be considered as much as village units as constructions with strong symbolic and ideological value, If the transmission of the architectural expression from Portugal and Andalousia immediately raises reservations, yet, correlations exist through a community of symbols.

At this phase the phenomenon of enclosures does not establish a link with the presence of the necropolis, the latter not being clearly attested at this final phase of the Neolithic. The indications gathered underline the non-defensive role of the enclosures. The Fontbuxian enclosures in stone of the hinterland are not very numerous and date rather to the terminal phase of this Culture; some are even reoccupied by populations of the Beaker tradition or early Bronze Age. Formal rapports, still to be fully demonstrated, exist between the Languedocian enclosures in stone and the Iberian walled enclosures. The latter are inscribed in the general context of diffusion and collection of vital resources and of social tension and the necessity of a territorial extension to the limits of exploited lands.

The extensive earthworks are dispositions for delimitation linked to the necessity of folding animals and protection of crops, whilst isolating the habitation site. The hypothesis currently held in honour puts in perspective two specific uses: a reproductive function of an architectural model with a cultural and social value and the need for territorial extension across the operating territories.

Conclusion

The occupation of the land is at first the exploit of small mobile communities of agro-pastoralists who leave few visible traces of their habitation site and construct megalithic monumental tombs, or not, which are sometimes grouped in a necropolis. It can be suggested that the anchorage of these communities and the probable affirmation of lineages are expressed essentially by emblematic funerary monuments. In a second phase, sepulchral practices diversify. The tombs group together on the living spaces, replacing them or setting them aside by reinvesting in old funerary emplacements. The habitation site becomes dense and there is a generalization of enclosures in the last third of the third millennium. These realizations, which depend on segmentary conception of architecture express the territorial anchorage of the new communities. Finally, for the same reason as the dry-stone hamlets with joined up houses, the enclosures site of eastern Languedoc express the identity of the Fontbouisse culture. The population's density deduced from the considerable number of settlements as well as a long mastery of construction techniques gave these societies the technical means to increase the wide range of their realizations. This no longer concerns tombs, which rarely require the edification of an ostentatious monument but more or less elaborated delimitations dispositions. This evolution expresses the valorization of lands and an extension of commons exploited by the agro-pastoralists accompanying the socializing function of place. This simplifying schema can hardly be surpassed in the state of terrain data. The balancing movement between necropolis and enclosure (Fig. 2B) expresses all the more the valorization of land and the extension of commons in a perspective of the socialization of the landscape.

Bibliography

AMBERT, P. 2006. La métallurgie pré-campaniforme dans le midi de la France (Grands causses, Languedoc central). In Gasco, J., Leyge, J., Gruat, P., dir. – Hommes et passé des Causses, hommage à Georges Costantini, Actes du Colloque de Millau 16-18 juin 2005. Toulouse: Edition des Archives d'Écologie Préhistoriques, p. 181-204.

AMBERT, P.; COULAROU, J.; CERT, C.; GUENDON, J. L.; BOURGARIT, D.; DAINAT, D.; HOULÈS, N.; BAUMES, B. 2002. Le plus vieil établissement de métallurgistes de France (IIIe millénaire av. J.-C): Péret (Hérault). C. R. Paléovol. 1:1, p. 67-74.

ARNAL, J. 1973. Le Lébous à Saint-Mathieu-de-Tréviers (Hérault). Ensemble du Chalcolithique au Gallo-Romain, 1, Étude archéologique. Gallia Préhistoire. 16:1, p. 131-193.

CANET, H.; ROUDIL, J.-L. 1978. Le village chalcolithique de Cambous (Viols-en-Laval, Hérault). Gallia Préhistoire. 21:1, p. 143-188.

CARDOSO, J. L. 1997. Genese, apogeu e declinio das fortificaçoes calcolíticas da Extramadura, Origin, Apogee and Decline of the Chalcolithic Fortifications in the Portuguese Extramadura. Zephyrus. 50, p. 249-261.

CAROZZA, L.; GEORJON, C.; VIGNAUD, A., eds. 2005. La fin des temps néolithiques et les débuts de la métallurgie en Languedoc central. Les habitats de la colline du Puech Haut à Paulhan, Hérault. Toulouse: Edition des Archives d'Ecologie Préhistorique/EHESS, 666 p.

COLOMER, A.; COULAROU, J.; GUTHERZ, X., eds. 1990. Boussargues (Argelliers, Hérault): un habitat ceinturé chalcolithique: les fouilles du secteur ouest. Paris: Maison des Sciences de l'Homme, 224 p. (Documents d'Archéologie Française; 24).

COULAROU, J.; JALLET, F.; COLOMER, A.; BALBURE, J. 2008. Boussargues: une enceinte chalcolithique des garrigues du Sud de la France. Toulouse: EHESS, 337 p.

DIÀZ-DEL-RIO, P. 2008. El context social de las agregaciones de población durante el Calcolítico Peninsular. ERA Arqueologia, 8. Lisboa: Era-Arqueologia / Colibri. p. 128-137.

GASCÓ, J. 1976. La communauté paysanne de Fontbouisse. Carcassonne: Laboratoire de Préhistoire et Palethnologie, 121 p.

GUILAINE, J. 1997. Les débuts de la métallurgie du cuivre en Méditerranée occidentale. Questions ouvertes, hypothèses archéologiques. In Ambert, P. ed.- Actes du colloque 'Mines et métallurgies de la Préhistoire au Moyen-Âge en Languedoc-Roussillon et régions périphériques'. Cabrières, 16-19 mai 1997, p. 9-15. (Archéologie en Languedoc; n°21).

GUTHERZ, X. 1975. La culture de Fontbouisse: recherches sur le chalcolithique en Languedoc oriental. ARALO: Caveirac, 120 p. (Association pour la recherche Archéologique en Languedoc oriental; cahier n°2).

GUTHERZ, X.; DUDAY, H.; VAQUER, J. 2010. Les sépultures néolithiques dans le Midi méditerranéen: cinquante ans d'études. In Delestre, X.; Marchesi, H., eds. – Archéologie des rivages méditerranéens: 50 ans de recherche. Actes du colloque d'Arles (Bouches-du-Rhône), 28-29-30 octobre 2009. Paris: Errance/Ministère de la Culture et de la Communication, p. 407-417.

GUTHERZ, X.; JALLOT, L. 1989. Les habitats chalcolithiques ceinturés de l'Hérault oriental. In D'Anna, A.; Gutherz, X., eds. – Enceintes, habitats ceinturés et sites perchés du Néolithique au Bronze ancien dans le sud de la France et les régions voisines. Actes de la table-ronde de Lattes et Aix-en-Provence, 15-18 avril 1987. Montpellier, p. 111-126. (Mémoires de la Soc. Lang. de Préhistoire; 2).

GUTHERZ, X.; JALLOT, L. 1995. Le Néolithique final du Languedoc méditerranéen. In Voruz, J.-L., ed. – Chronologies néolithiques, de 6000 ans à 2000 ans avant notre ère dans le Bassin rhodanien. Ambérieu-en-Bugey, 19-20 septembre 1992. Ambérieu-en-Bugey: Ed. Société préhistorique rhodanienne, p. 213-263. (Doc. du Dépt. d'Anthropologie de l'Université de Genève; n°20).

GUTHERZ, X.; JALLOT, L. 1999. Approche géoculturelle des pays fontbuxiens. In Vaquer J., ed – Le Néolithique du Nord-Ouest méditerranéen, XXIVe Congrès Préhistorique de France, Carcassonne, 26-30 septembre 1994. Paris: SPF, p. 161-174.

GUTHERZ, X.; JALLOT, L.; WATTEZ, C.; BORGNON, C.; ROUX, J.-C.; THOUVENOT, Y.; ORGEVAL, M. 2011. L'habitat néolithique final de la Capoulière IV (Mauguio, Hérault): présentation des principaux résultats 2004-2007. In Senepart, I.; Perrin, T.; Thirault, E.; Bonnardin S., eds. – Marges, frontières et transgressions, actualité de la recherché. Actes des 8e Rencontres Méridionales de Préhistoire Récente, Marseille, 7 et 8 novembre 2008. Toulouse: Archives d'Ecologie Préhistorique, p. 413-438.

HASLER, A.; CHEVILLOT, P.; COLLET, H.; DURAND, C.; RENAULT, S.; RICHIER, A. 1998. La nécropole tumulaire néolithique de Château Blanc (Ventabren, Bouches-du-Rhône). In D'Anna, A; Binder,

D., eds. – Production et identité culturelle. Actes des IIe Rencontres Méridionales de Préhistoire Récente, Arles, nov. 1996. Antibes: APDCA, p. 403-414.

JALLOT, L. 1990. Conservation et distribution du matériel céramique: de l'espace domestique à l'espace social. In Colomer, A.; Coularou, J.; Gutherz, X., eds. – Boussargues (Argelliers, Hérault): un habitat ceinturé chalcolithique: les fouilles du secteur ouest. Paris: Maison des Sciences de l'Homme, p. 171-197. (Documents d'Archéologie Française; 24).

JALLOT, L. 2003. Le groupe de Ferrières dans l'Hérault et la question du 'style des Vautes'. In Guilaine, J.; Escallon, G., eds. – Les Vautes (Saint-Gély-du-Fesc, Hérault) et le Néolithique final du Languedoc oriental. Toulouse: Archives d'écologie préhistorique, p. 235-244.

JALLOT, L. 2010. La fin du Néolithique dans la moitié sud de la France. In Clottes J., dir. – La France préhistorique, un essai d'histoire. Paris: Ed. Gallimard, p. 361-379.

JALLOT, L. 2011. Frontières, stabilités, emprunts et dynamique géoculturelle en Languedoc méditerranéen au Néolithique final (3400-2300 av. J.-C.). In Sénépart, I.; Perrin, T.; Thirault, E.; Bonnardin, S., eds. – Marges, frontières et transgressions, actualité de la recherche, Actes des 8e Rencontres Méridionales de Préhistoire Récente, Marseille, 7 et 8 novembre 2008. Toulouse: Archives d'Ecologie Préhistorique, p. 87-119.

JALLOT, L. 2014. Le site de la colline Saint-Michel (Montpellier, Languedoc): la question de la transition Néolithique final 2-3. In Senepart, I.; Léandri, F.; Cauliez, J.; Perrin, T.; Thirault, E., eds. – Chronologie de la Préhistoire récente dans le Sud de la France. Actualité de la recherche, Actes des 10e Rencontres Méridionales de Préhistoire Récente, Porticcio (Corse), 18-22 octobre 2012. Toulouse: Archives d'Ecologie Préhistorique, p. 87-135.

JALLOT, L., ed. 2004. Le Mas de Vignoles IV à Nîmes (Gard), Document Final de Synthèse. AFAN, SRA Languedoc-Roussillon, 2 volumes, 13 fascicules, 1360 p.

LAPORTE, L.; JALLOT, L.; SOHN, M. 2011. Mégalithisme en France. Nouveaux acquis et nouvelles perspectives de recherche. Gallia Préhistoire. 53, p. 289-338.

LEMERCIER, O. 2004. Les Campaniformes dans le sud-est de la France. Lattes: UMR 154/ADAL, 515 p. (Monographies d'Archéologie Méditerranéenne, n°18).

Chapter 3

Southern Europe: Spain and Portugal

Prehistoric ditched enclosures and necropolises in Southern Iberia: a diachronic overview

Víctor JIMÉNEZ-JÁIMEZ
Marie Curie IEF Post-Doctoral Researcher, Archaeology, University of Southampton,
Avenue Campus, SO17 1BF Southampton, United Kingdom
V.J.Jimenez-Jaimez@soton.ac.uk

José Enrique MÁRQUEZ-ROMERO
Área de Prehistoria, Departamento de Ciencias y Técnicas Historiográficas,
Historia Antigua y Prehistoria, Universidad de Málaga, Campus de Teatinos,
s/n 29071 Málaga, Spain
jemarquez@uma.es

Abstract

In this paper, we shall briefly describe the main features of Southern Iberian Final Neolithic and Copper Age enclosures, and will examine how they relate in space and time to Prehistoric funerary contexts. We will attempt to show how this relationship changed through time. In the 4th millennium BC, during the Final Neolithic, both megalithic tombs and ditched enclosures were built. However, very rarely they are close in space. In the 3rd millennium BC, coinciding with the Chalcolithic, necropolises of tombs (tholoi and hypogea) began to form around ditched enclosures of the period. However, this process only occurred at a few sites – the 'mega-sites'.

Keywords: *Archaeology, funerary practices, human remains, pits, megalithic tombs, ditched enclosures, Neolithic, Copper Age, Iberian Peninsula*

Résumé

Dans ce article, nous allons décrire brièvement les principales formes d'enceintes du Néolithique récent et du Chacolithique du sud de la péninsule ibérique et nous examinerons leurs relations dans l'espace et le temps avec les contextes funéraires contemporains. Nous montrerons comment ces relations changent au cours du temps. Au cours du 4e millénaire avant notre ère, au Néolithique récent, des tombes mégalithiques ainsi que des enceintes fossoyées sont construites en même temps mais rarement à proximité. Au 3e millénaire, au cours du Chalcolithique, des nécropoles funéraires composées de tholoi et d'hypogées commencent à se former autour de certaines enceintes: les 'méga-sites'.

Mots-clés: *Archeologie, pratiques funéraires, restes humains, fosses, tombes mégalithiques, enceintes fossoyées, Néolithique, Chalcolithique, péninsule ibérique*

Introduction

Neolithic and Copper Age ditched enclosures (4th-3rd millennia BC) are one of the hottest topics in Iberian Prehistory today (e.g. see Márquez-Romero and Jiménez-Jáimez 2013). They have been found in almost all Iberian regions, but there seems to be a higher concentration in the central plateau (*Meseta Central*), the East (*Levante*) and, particularly, the South, where most fieldwork has been carried out, and where the focus of this paper will be (Fig. 1). Since their discovery in the 1970s, Southern Iberian ditched enclosures have been interpreted mainly as fortified villages defended by ditches and other non-surviving above ground elements such as palisades or banks. These so-called fortifications were supposedly built and inhabited by large groups that lived all year round within the limits defined by the ditches (e.g. Lizcano *et al.* 1991-1992; Arteaga and Cruz-Auñón 1999; Cruz-Auñón and Arteaga 1999; Nocete 2001; Morán and Parreira 2003; Cámara *et al.* 2011). Only in the

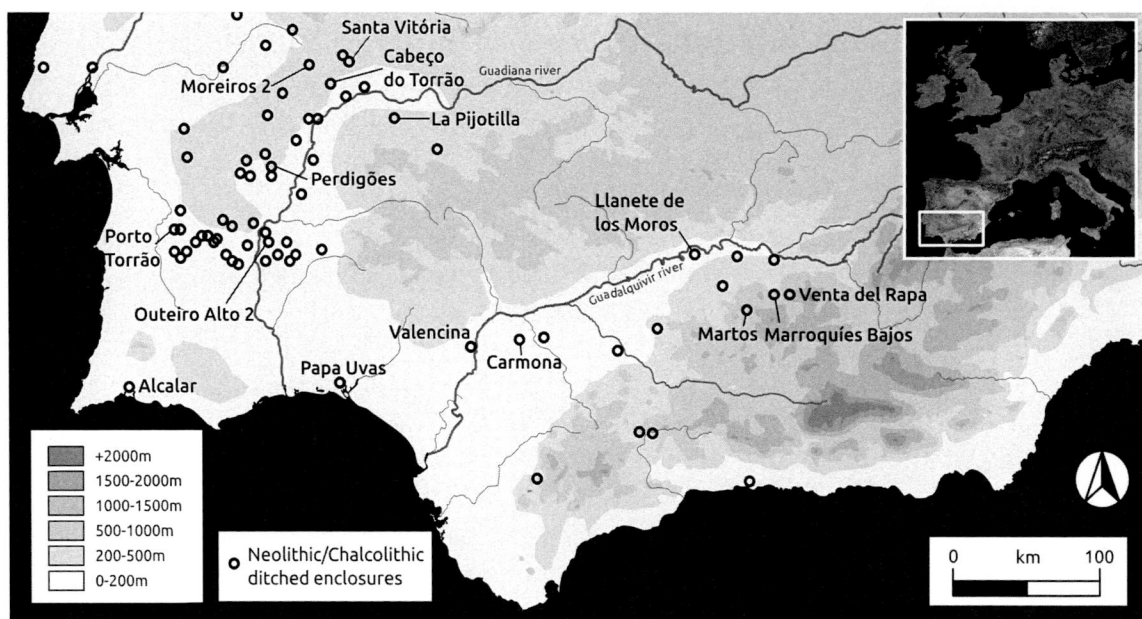

FIGURE 1. MAPS SHOWING THE GEOGRAPHICAL DISTRIBUTION OF NEOLITHIC AND COPPER AGE DITCHED ENCLOSURES IN SOUTHERN IBERIA, WITH INDICATION OF THE SITES MENTIONED IN THE TEXT (BACKGROUND SATELLITE IMAGE OF EUROPE BY RETO STÖCKLI, NASA EARTH OBSERVATORY).

last 12 years this interpretation has been challenged, on the basis of little attention paid to issues of temporality and formation of the archaeological record, ambiguous evidence of stable occupation of the inner areas at many enclosures or questions about the defensive capabilities of said places and the structures that circumscribe them (e.g. Márquez-Romero 2003; 2006; Martín de la Cruz and Lucena 2003; Márquez-Romero and Jiménez-Jáimez 2010, 2013; Valera 2012a; García Sanjuán and Murillo-Barroso 2013).

Where Southern Iberian Prehistoric ditched enclosures are conceived as places occupied throughout the year, the relationship between them and contemporary necropolises – chiefly megalithic – may seem straightforward: they would represent a dualistic organisation of space within a settlement, with an area devoted to daily life and activities – the village or town –, separated from another one reserved for funerary rituals – the necropolis or cemetery. History and anthropology, however, show that this duality between the living and the dead, and particularly the distribution of space in terms of the opposition of the sacred and the profane, or the ritual and the everyday, is typically Western, and does not necessarily apply to other cultural contexts (Brück 1999). If the conceptualisation of Southern Iberian ditched enclosures as fortified and permanently inhabited settlements is questioned, and instead more fluid or mobile lifestyles and settlement patterns are proposed (see above), then the issue becomes even more problematic. These questions are underlined by the Final Neolithic and Chalcolithic Southern Iberian evidence itself, for most ditched enclosures do not have an associated necropolis in their proximity.

In this paper, we shall briefly describe the main features of Southern Iberian Final Neolithic and Copper Age enclosures, and will examine how they relate in space and time to funerary contexts. Before we attempt to do that, a clarification involving the concept of 'necropolis' used here needs to be made, nonetheless. Often at Southern Iberian ditched enclosures two contrasting phenomena occur:
   a. The discovery of human remains in dedicated containers, such as megalithic or rock-cut tombs, often accompanied with what archaeologists have traditionally termed grave goods.

b. The recording of complete bodies, body parts or isolated bones recovered from ditches, pits and other non-dedicated contexts. Here, the presence of human remains does not appear to be essential, but contingent upon other conditions being met; pits and ditches containing human remains are actually a minority relative to the totality of such features.

This dichotomy could even have a spatial component. For example, at Porto Torrão (Ferreira do Alentejo, Portugal), there seems to be a clear contrast in the distribution of features including human bones. Collective burials following a normalised funerary ritual in tombs, which constitute the majority of contexts with human bones at the site, are located outside the ditched enclosures. By contrast, pits containing osteological remains, much more scarce, are located inside the enclosed areas (Rodrigues 2014). Of course, there are grey areas, and the evidence from other sites may show different patterns. It all could very well end up being a continuum of practices involving the human body, of which we are seeing only the two extremes. But we believe it is worth considering the possibility that, overall, the differences between 'a' and 'b' could be indicative of two or more distinctive practices or behaviours in the past. It is important to note, however, that we do not see the binary character of the evidence as described here as a materialisation of the typically Western dichotomies of the sacred and the profane; the meaning of this distinction is much more subtle, complex and difficult for us to grasp than that.

For pragmatic reasons, not least of which is to make our point more evident, in this paper we will restrict the use of the concept of 'necropolis' to only a subset of all the contexts in which human remains are found, coinciding with phenomenon 'a' above. Thus, we will consider a necropolis a cluster of dedicated funerary containers with some kind of normalised shape, size and building technique. These structures must contain human bones (or it must be suspected that at some point they did), and in them the human body has to be the most important element of the rite, its *raison d'être*, the centre of attention. That should be reflected in a dominant position within the funerary container, in quantitative, or especially, qualitative terms. Although not essential, a common feature of funerary contexts is the appearance of grave goods, that is, an assemblage of items which can directly be associated with the bodies, supposedly deposited to accompany the deceased in their transition to the world of the dead, following existing guidelines or traditions. We are aware of the somewhat arbitrary character of this definition, and we see it more as a provisional working hypothesis worth exploring than as a true fact; the conclusions reached will therefore have to be taken as such (see also Márquez-Romero and Jiménez-Jáimez 2014).

Unfortunately, data is still fragmentary in many cases, particularly as regards the size of the enclosures and the layout of the ditches. Further, the quantity and quality of available dates does not yet come close to that of other European regions such as Britain (Whittle *et al.* 2011), and is often clearly insufficient to understand the relationship in time between different elements of the archaeological record like ditches, pits, walls, houses and tombs. It is nevertheless good enough to support the idea that Iberian ditched enclosures were a long-lasting phenomenon in the Prehistory of the Iberian Peninsula. Perhaps for that reason, ditched enclosures are quite diverse in their defining characteristics and probably their social roles. Therefore, they, and the relationship between them and the necropolises of the same period, must be understood in time. This paper will hence address these issues following a chronological sequence.

1. Final Neolithic ditched enclosures and necropolises in Iberia (last three centuries of the 4th millennium BC)

The earliest known ditched enclosures in Southern Iberia thus far date back to last three centuries of the fourth millennium cal BC (Márquez Romero and Jiménez Jáimez 2010: 198-204, 2013: 455; Valera 2013: 338; Boaventura and Mataloto 2013: 86). Moreiros 2 (Portalegre, Portugal) (Boaventura 2006; Valera *et al.* 2013a), Cabeço do Torrão (Elvas, Portugal) (Lago and Albergaria 2001), Llanete de los Moros (Córdoba, Spain) (Martín de la Cruz 1987) and the earlier acts of ditch-digging at

Perdigões (Reguengos de Monsaraz, Portugal) (Lago *et al*. 1998; Márquez *et al*. 2011; Valera *et al*. 2014), Porto Torrão (Beja, Portugal) (Valera and Filipe 2004; Rodrigues 2014); Papa Uvas (Huelva, Spain) (Martín de la Cruz and Lucena 2003), and Martos (Jaén, Spain) (Lizcano *et al*. 1991-1992; Lizcano 1999) are the ones which provided more information so far.

Southern Iberian Final Neolithic ditched enclosures were often located in river basins like those of Guadiana and Guadalquivir. Generally speaking, they do not present traces of houses or walls; usually only structures dug in the ground (enclosing ditches, pits) are documented, with sporadic instances of possible foundation trenches for timber palisades. Data about their layout is fragmentary and incomplete in most cases, but they appear to have been concentric circular or oval spaces, sometimes with somewhat straight sides, delimited by ditches. The ditches are often non-causewayed, with the exception of few entrances, ie spots where the ditches are interrupted, allowing access in or out of the enclosed space. Some of the ditches are wavy or sinuous (Valera 2012a). The size of the enclosed areas varies from less than 1 ha to around 10 ha, while the dimensions of the ditches range from 1 m to 6 m in width and 1 m to 3 m in depth, although the average Final Neolithic ditch would be around 2 m wide and 2 m deep. The profile of the ditches is normally either U or V-shaped. Most pits are approximately circular, 1 to 2 m in both depth and diameter. In broad terms, enclosures from this period appear to have shared the Neolithic landscapes of Southern Iberia with other elements –i.e pit sites, lithic scatters, schematic art places and, of course, funerary contexts. Regarding this, megalithic (*dolmens*, *antas*) and rock-cut tombs (*hypogea* or 'artificial caves') holding collective inhumations constitute the main forms of burial throughout the period.

There is only one Southern Iberian site dated in this period where a clear relation of proximity between a ditched enclosure and a megalithic or rock-cut funerary structure has been observed. That is Cabeço do Torrão (Barbacena, Elvas, Portugal). Located in a flat, low hill but with good visibility over its surroundings, excavations carried out in the late 1990s detected a ditch and 14 pits. The ditch is V-shaped, 1 m deep and 1,5 m wide at the most, and describes a small enclosure of less than 1 ha. No radiocarbon dates have been obtained, but the typologies of the ceramic materials unearthed suggest a Final Neolithic chronology for the ditch and most of the pits. 15 small menhirs or standing stones were found immediately SW of the ditch, and over 100 m further in the same direction a small *anta* (megalithic funerary chamber) containing Neolithic material was identified and excavated. However, there are problems with the association between the enclosure and the anta. Simply put, at the moment there is no way to know if both structures were in use simultaneously (Lago and Albergaria 2001: 60).

Cabeço do Torrão is, at best, a weak exception to a more general pattern consisting on the non-proximity of ditched enclosures and megalithic burials in the 4th millennium BC. In fact, most Final Neolithic ditched enclosures elsewhere in Southern Iberia do not show a direct association with megalithic tombs. Some indirect relationships can be seen, nonetheless. Perdigões (Reguengos de Monsaraz, Portugal) (Lago *et al*. 1998) is a good example. The site comprises no fewer than 12 roughly concentric ditched rings, some of them wavy ditches, with at least one palisade (inner circle) and thousands of pits (Márquez-Romero *et al*. 2011). Ditches and pits are of diverse chronologies, from the Final Neolithic to the Late Copper Age (second half of the 4th millennium to the last third of the 3rd millennium cal BC) (Valera *et al*. 2014). To the E of the enclosures there is also an area with several Copper Age tombs and a cluster of standing stones (*cromeleque*). The site as a whole occupies an area of about 16 ha. For now we will focus on the Final Neolithic evidence only (ditch 5, probably ditch 8, and especially ditches 12 and 6, enclosing an area of just over 1 ha, as well as a few pits), thus momentarily ignoring the Chalcolithic necropolis and enclosures.

Perdigões is located near the right bank of the Ribeira do Álamo valley, a tributary of the Guadiana river. The valley is rich in Neolithic megalithic tombs (antas) that have been known for a long time (Leisner and Leisner 1951; Gonçalves 1992). The chronology of these structures is sometimes unknown or unreliable, but it is very likely that when the earliest ditched circuits were constructed

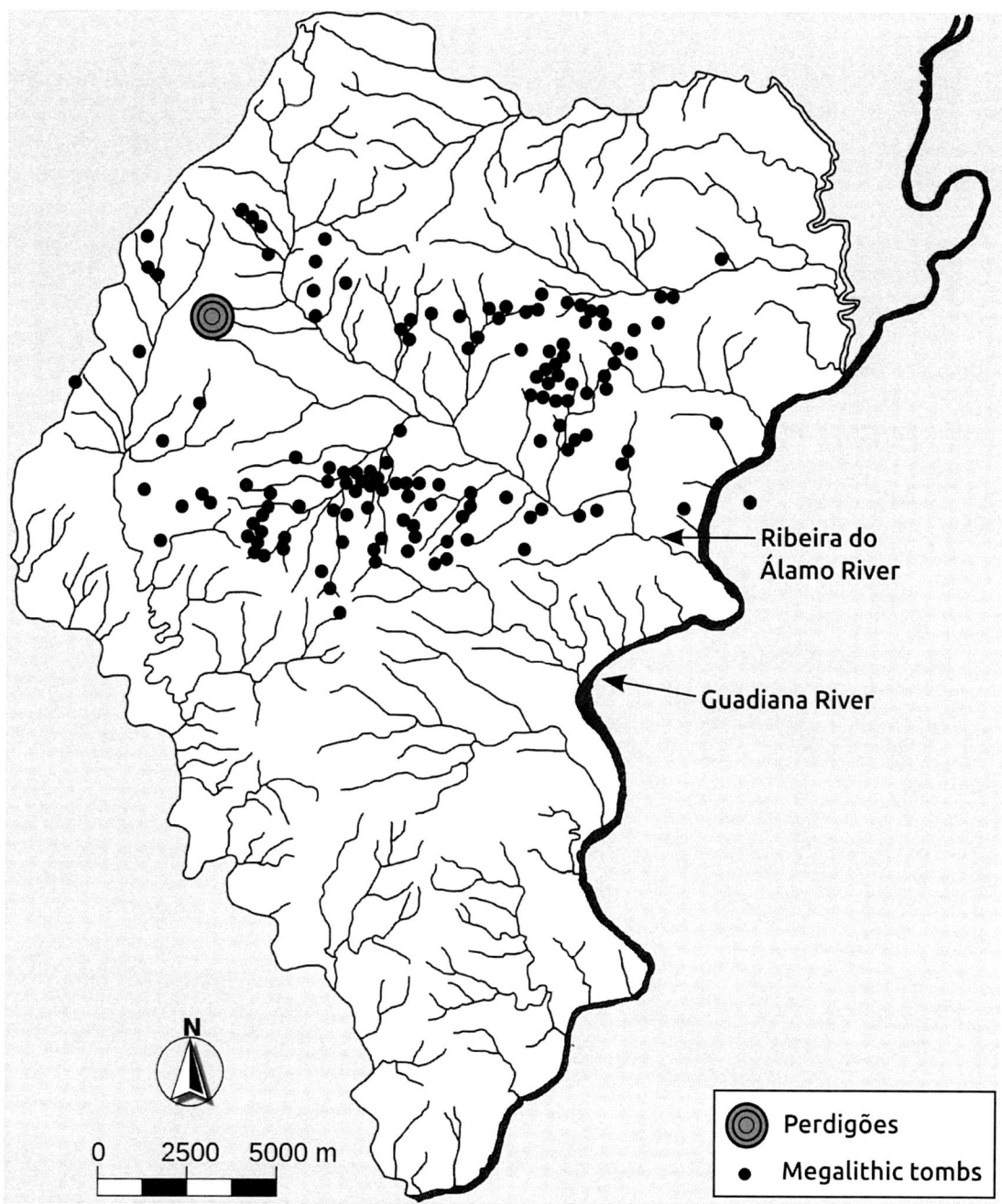

FIGURE 2. PERDIGÕES (REGUENGOS DE MONSARAZ, PORTUGAL) AND ITS SPATIAL RELATIONS WITH NEOLITHIC MEGALITHIC TOMBS (*ANTAS*) WITHIN THE LANDSCAPE SURROUNDING THE RIBEIRA DO ÁLAMO RIVER (MODIFIED FROM VALERA 2006, FIG. 3). IT IS A GOOD EXAMPLE OF THE INDIRECT CONNECTIONS BETWEEN DITCHED ENCLOSURES AND NECROPOLISES IN THE FINAL NEOLITHIC (4TH MILLENNIUM CAL BC) IN SOUTHERN IBERIA.

at Perdigões, numerous antas were already populating the valley (Fig. 2). Crucially, Perdigões is not only located on the margins of a valley with plenty of Neolithic megalithic burials: the local topography of the place is also naturally oriented towards them. Perdigões is characterised by a gentle slope descending from W to E. The N and the S of the place are also higher than the centre of the ditched enclosures. It all results in a basin-like shape, or even better, a Greek theatre: from the centre of the site visibility is almost non-existent to the N, the S and the W. Visibility is, however, good to the E, which is where the menhirs are located and the valley begins and, with it, the megalithic tombs spread throughout the lands that lead to the Guadiana river.

Currently available evidence from sites like Moreiros 2, Porto Torrão, Papa Uvas, Llanete de los Moros or Martos (see references above), among others, suggest that, with its peculiarities, Perdigões is a paradigmatic example of the dynamics of the Late 4th millennium BC in the region: megalithic or rock-cut tombs did not form necropolises near ditched enclosures during the Final Neolithic in Southern Iberia. Instead, they were more or less dispersed across the landscape, and the relationships between enclosures and necropolis were indirect. For example, no megalithic burials were recorded in the immediate surroundings of the Moreiros 2 ditched enclosures (Arronches, Portalegre, Portugal). However, an anta sits 1 km away to the NE. Interestingly, visibility to and from the site is restricted in most directions, but less so to the NE, towards the megalithic tomb (Boaventura 2006: 68).

In contrast with this, even though most Southern Iberian Final Neolithic ditched enclosures have not been extensively surveyed, they are known to abound in pits. Of those pits, a relatively small percentage, located either within the boundaries created by the enclosing ditches or in their proximity, contain human bones or complete bodies. That is the case, for example, of a few pits at Llanete de los Moros (Martín de la Cruz 1987, p. 48), Perdigões (Valera and Godinho 2009; Valera and Silva 2011: 11) or Martos (Lizcano *et al*. 1991-1992: 21). In our view, these instances should not be mistaken for necropolises or cemeteries. Unlike what we would normally expect from a necropolis, in all these sites pits are numerous but those with human bones are few; they appear to be the exception and not the rule. Further, the presence of human remains does not fundamentally alter the content of the pits. Whether they include human bones or not, most pits usually hold complex assemblages comprising a variable combination of stone blocks of varied types and sizes, artefacts such as ceramic sherds, flint tools and knapping waste or quern stones, often broken or incomplete, as well as animal remains, both complete and articulated carcasses and isolated bones or body parts. Moreover, although the sample size is still small, it seems that the arrangement of osteological remains within the pits is not normalised, and no clear-cut grave goods can be recognised.

2. Chalcolithic (3rd millennium BC) ditched enclosures and necropolises in Iberia

In the third millennium cal BC (Chalcolithic/Copper Age) the general picture turned more complicated in Iberia. Ditched enclosures continued to be built arguably until the last few centuries of the millennium (Márquez Romero and Jiménez Jáimez 2010: 204-208, 2013: 455; Valera 2013: 339). However, both the sites themselves and the landscapes they populated evolved.

There is reason to believe that the main heyday of the Southern Iberian ditched enclosure tradition occurred during the Copper Age. The main characteristics of Iberian ditched enclosures mentioned above, –ie tendency to circularity, concentric, continuous and often sinuous ditches, scarcity of undisputed evidence of houses or walls, profusion of pits, depositional practices, etc.– remained more or less constant, at least for most sites. Examples of this are Outeiro Alto 2 (Serpa, Portugal) (Valera *et al*. 2013b), Santa Vitória (Portalegre, Portugal) (cited in Hurtado 2008: 192), Venta del Rapa (Jaén, Spain) (Lechuga *et al*. 2014), or the late acts of ditch-digging at Papa Uvas (see references above), amongst many others. The general impression, therefore, is not one of structural change but of continuity. However, the social forces that led to the construction of ditched enclosures, whatever they were, not only continued but intensified even further, as reflected in the appearance of a few larger sites with truly monumental features. That is the case of Valencina de la Concepción (Seville, Spain) (Vargas 2004; García Sanjuán *et al*. 2013), La Pijotilla (Badajoz, Spain) (Hurtado 1986, 1999, 2008), Alcalar (Portimão, Portugal) (Morán and Parreira 2003), Marroquíes Bajos (Jaén, Spain) (Zafra *et al*. 1999, 2003) and later phases of building activity at Perdigões and Porto Torrão (see references above), which show unique characteristics. At those 'mega-sites', interior areas substantially increased. Thus, the outer ditch at Marroquíes Bajos enclosed an estimated area of over 100 ha, La Pijotilla 70 ha, Alcalar 20 ha and Perdigões 16 ha, while Chalcolithic features are spread across vast areas of more than 400 ha at Valencina de la Concepción and Porto Torrão – including their extensive necropolises, as we will see below –. The ditches also grew, reaching up to 9 m or even 20 m in width and 7 m in depth on occasions. Even the pits seem to be generally larger.

Pit sites and other characteristic elements of the Final Neolithic landscapes persisted. However, certain aspects of the cultural landscapes appear to dramatically change at the beginning of the Copper Age period. In particular, the 3rd millennium cal BC saw the advent of new architectural principles in the form of stone-walled enclosures, with 'towers' and 'bastion-like' features, akin to the well-known south-eastern site of Los Millares (e.g. Molina *et al.* 2004; Jorge 1994). Restricted geographically largely to the Iberian *Atlantic Façade* and the Southeast, stone-walled enclosures include what appear to be circular houses and other domestic features. The geographical distributions of ditched and walled enclosures partially overlap each other. In the absence of detailed chronologies, it is commonly assumed that they somehow shared the same spaces in certain areas of the Iberian Peninsula during these centuries.

At some point during the 3rd millennium BC, circular, stone-based houses, and stone masonry walls similar to those typical of the aforementioned walled enclosures, including towers and bastion-like features, began to appear at some of the 'mega' ditched enclosures (e.g. Alcalar or Marroquíes Bajos), although their chronology and therefore their relationship with ditches and pits often remain unclear. Metal artefacts, amongst other novel material culture items, appear on the archaeological record corresponding to this period.

The practice of deposition of human bones, body parts or complete skeletons in pits not only continued but increased, especially at, but not limited to, the 'mega' enclosures. Likewise, some sites saw the deposition of human remains in ditches. In both cases, and looking at the available data, there does not appear to be any kind of normalisation, and the diversity of sex and age distributions, anatomical conditions of the bodies, positions, treatment of the bones and accompanying objects, if any, is considerable (see e.g. Márquez-Romero and Jiménez-Jáimez 2010: 213-219; Valera 2012b). At least at some sites, these practices remained numerically less important than burials in tombs (again, see for example Rodrigues 2014 for Porto Torrão), but more data is needed to sustain this inference at a more general level (see e.g. García Sanjuán and Díaz-Zorita Bonilla 2013 for Valencina; and Valera, this volume, for Perdigões).

As regards normalised burials, a 'second megalithic tradition' featuring corbelled dome tombs, normally with a corridor and a circular chamber, called *tholoi*, materialised (García Sanjuán 2009: 18). At the same time, rock-cut tombs (hypogea) remained to be constructed, whilst the use and re-use of old mortuary monuments continued (Boaventura 2011). More importantly for the objectives of this paper, in Southern Iberia some of these forms of burials (tholoi, hypogea) formed necropolises nearby Chalcolithic ditched enclosures, or viceversa. Intra-site temporality is a big issue here: the contemporaneity of most of these features remains undemonstrated, and things that are close in space today not necessarily were close in time in the past. If the model proposed by Whittle *et al.* (2011) for Early Neolithic Britain is any indication, it is unlikely that Iberian ditched enclosures were constructed without a break for almost 1500 years, from the Final Neolithic to the Late Chalcolithic; instead, short bursts of building activity might have alternated with periods of relative inactivity on that front. If that is true also in Southern Iberia, the funerary structures mentioned above could have been built in-between episodes of ditch-digging. However, the British model does not necessarily apply to Southern Iberia as is, and Iberian chronologies do not allow yet to make inferences of that nature. Moreover, the proximity of tombs and ditched enclosures at some sites, regardless of the diachronic or synchronic character of their relationship, is a novelty of the period that deserves attention in itself, particularly when compared to the Final Neolithic.

Another important aspect of this is the restricted nature of the phenomenon. There are about 30 Chalcolithic ditched sites in Southern Iberia – counting just once the sites that have multiple Copper Age ditches such as Perdigões or La Pijotilla –, and many more are probable. Of those, only 6, maybe 7, have Chalcolithic necropolises in their proximity: La Pijotilla, Perdigões, Porto Torrão, Alcalar, Valencina de la Concepción, Marroquíes Bajos (see references above) and perhaps Carmona (Seville, Spain), where, according to several sources, a *tholos* was found in the 19th century (Conlin

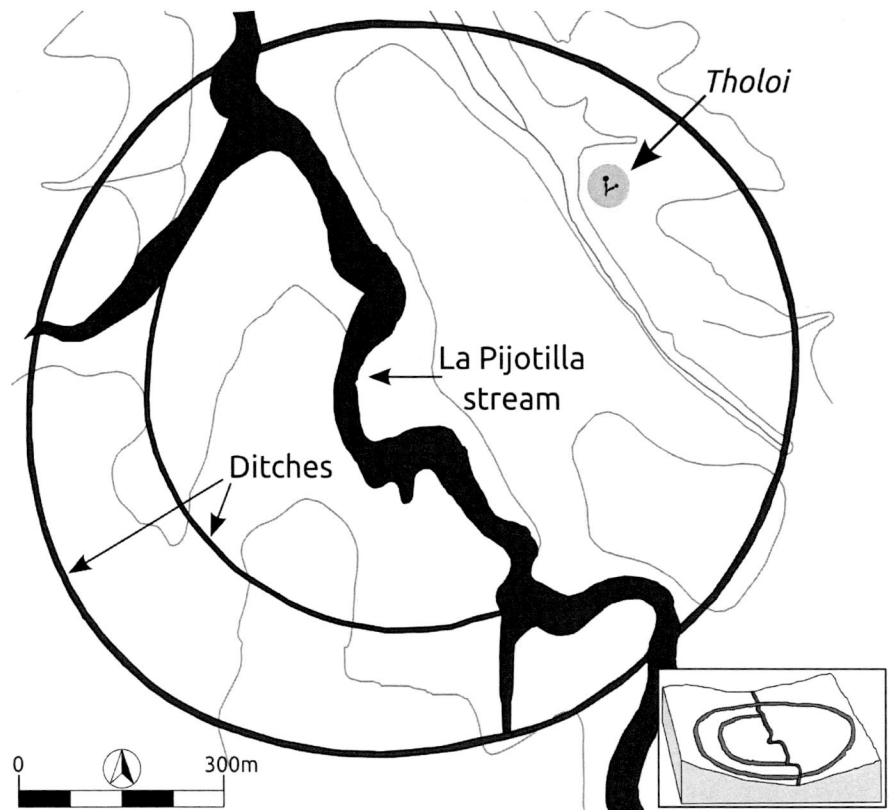

FIGURE 3. FLOOR PLAN OF LA PIJOTILLA (BADAJOZ) DITCHED ENCLOSURE, SPLIT INTO TWO HALVES BY A STREAM. THE NECROPOLIS, FEATURING SEVERAL THOLOI AND SOME SIMPLER FORMS, IS TODAY WITHIN THE ENCLOSED AREA, ALTHOUGH THE TEMPORALITY OF THE OUTER DITCH REMAINS UNCLEAR (MODIFIED FROM HURTADO 1999, FIG. 4). THIS ILLUSTRATES THE MUCH CLOSER CONNECTIONS BETWEEN (SOME) DITCHED ENCLOSURES AND NECROPOLISES IN THE SOUTHERN IBERIAN COPPER AGE (3RD MILLENNIUM CAL BC).

2003: 87-88). Necropolises nearby Southern Iberian ditched enclosures are, therefore, unusual, even in the Chalcolithic. Importantly, the sites with clusters of tombs are also the largest and the ones which possess the most monumental features (ditches and pits) in the region. In other words, as far as Southern Iberian Copper Age ditched enclosures is concerned, only the 'mega-sites' were accompanied by necropolises.

Although simpler forms exist, the necropolises at the Copper Age 'mega-sites' commonly comprise tholoi and hypogea and usually contain collective inhumations. In a few instances, the outer ditch was constructed in such a way to include some pre-existing tombs in the enclosed area; this occurs at Perdigões (Valera *et al.* 2014: 20-21) and probably La Pijotilla (Hurtado 1986) (Fig. 3), although the chronology of the outer circuit at the latter is less certain. By contrast, at Valencina de la Concepción (Cruz-Auñón and Mejías 2013) and Porto Torrão (Valera *et al.* in press) the tombs appear to be spread across such wide areas that some funerary contexts are located several hundred metres, or even kilometres, away from the known ditches, and organised in several clusters. More and better surveys, leading to a more comprehensive understanding of the layout of the ditches, are needed, nonetheless.

Concluding remarks

Despite the evident shortcomings of the available data, in terms of spatial distribution of the evidence and, particularly, their temporality, some basic trends seem to be emerging in the archaeological record of the 4th and 3rd millennia BC in Southern Iberia. The changing nature of the relationship between necropolises and ditched enclosures throughout the period under study appears to be one of them. In the 4th millennium BC, during the Final Neolithic, both megalithic tombs and ditched enclosures were built. However, very rarely they are close in space. When ditched enclosures and tombs coincide in one region, e.g. the Ribeira do Álamo valley around Perdigões, the megalithic burials do not seem to cluster in the proximities of the enclosure. Quite the contrary, they are often distributed throughout the landscape, outside the enclosed spaces and almost always away from the ditches and their accompanying pits. Interestingly, some human remains, both body parts and whole carcasses, have been identified at ditched enclosures of the 4th millennium BC, but these are mostly restricted to a minority of pits. Hence, human bones found at ditched enclosures of this period were buried in non-monumental, non-dedicated containers distributed throughout non-specifically-funerary areas.

In the 3rd millennium BC, coinciding with the Chalcolithic, and in clear contrast with the Final Neolithic, necropolises of tombs (tholoi and hypogea) began to form around ditched enclosures of the period. However, this process only occurred at a few sites – the 'mega-sites' – that stand out from the rest because of their unique characteristics: large enclosed areas, monumental features (ditches and pits) and sometimes walls and houses. Moreover, the apparent association of ditched enclosures and dedicated funerary areas consisting of clusters of tombs should only be taken as valid when the simultaneity of their use is demonstrated with systematic radiocarbon dating programmes. Unfortunately, that is not the case for most sites at the moment, and the chronological relationships between ditches, pits, walls, tombs and houses often remain unclear.

Acknowledgements

The research leading to these results has received funding from the People Programme (Marie Curie Actions) of the European Union's Seventh Framework Programme (FP7/2007-2013) under REA grant agreement nº 2012-326129. It has also received funding from the Plan Nacional de I+D+I of the Ministerio de Economía y Competitividad of Spain (project number HAR2010-21610-C02-01).

Bibliography

ARTEAGA, O.; CRUZ-AUÑÓN, R. 1999. Una valoración del patrimonio histórico en el campo de silos de la finca El Cuervo-RTVA (Valencina de la Concepción, Sevilla). Excavación de urgencia de 1995. Anuario Arqueológico de Andalucía. Sevilla. 1995: 3, p. 608-616.
BOAVENTURA, R. 2006. Os IV e III milénio a.n.e. na região de Monforte, para além dos mapas com pontos: os casos do cluster de Rabuje e do povoado com fossos de Moreiros 2. Revista Portuguesa de Arqueologia, Lisbon. 9: 2, p. 61-73.
BOAVENTURA, R. 2011. Chronology of Megalithism in South Central Portugal. In García Sanjuán, L.; Scarre, C.; Wheatley, D., ed. – Exploring Time and Matter in Prehistoric Monuments: Absolute Chronology and Rare Rocks in European Megaliths. Antequera: Menga Monographic Series 1, p. 159-190.
BOAVENTURA, R.; MATALOTO, R. 2013. Entre mortos e vivos: nótulas acerca da cronologia absoluta do Megalitismo do Sul de Portugal. Revista Portuguesa de Arqueologia, Lisbon. 16, p. 81-101.
BRÜCK, J. 1999. Ritual and rationality: some problems of interpretation in European Archaeology. European Journal of Archaeology. 2: 3, p. 313-344.
CÁMARA, J. A.; SPANEDDA, L.; GÓMEZ DEL TORO, E.; LIZCANO, R. 2011. La discusión sobre la función de los fosos en la Prehistoria reciente del sur de la Península Ibérica. Modas y temores. In Abellán, J.; Castañeda, V., coord – Homenaje al profesor Antonio Caro Bellido. Cádiz: Universidad de Cádiz, Servicio de Publicaciones, p. 61-80.
CONLIN, E. 2003. Los inicios del III milenio a.C. en Carmona: las evidencias arqueológicas. Carel, Carmona. 1, p. 83-143.

Cruz-Auñón, R.; Arteaga, O. 1999. Acerca de un campo de silos y un foso de cierre prehistóricos ubicados en 'La Estacada Larga' (Valencina de la Concepción, Sevilla). Excavación de urgencia de 1995. Anuario Arqueológico de Andalucía. Sevilla. 1995: 3, p. 600-607.

Cruz-Auñón, R.; Mejías, J. C. 2013. Diversidad de prácticas funerarias e identidades en el asentamiento de Valencina de la Concepción (Sevilla). In García Sanjuán, L.; Vargas Jiménez, J. M.; Hurtado, V.; Ruiz Moreno, T.; Cruz-Auñón, R., ed – El asentamiento prehistórico de Valencina de la Concepción (Sevilla). Investigación y tutela en el 150 aniversario del descubrimiento de La Pastora. Sevilla: Universidad de Sevilla. p. 175-199.

García Sanjuán, L. 2009. Introducción a los sitios y paisajes megalíticos de Andalucía. In García Sanjuán, L.; Ruiz, B., ed – Las grandes piedras de la Prehistoria. Sitios y paisajes megalíticos de Andalucía. Antequera: Junta de Andalucía, p. 12-31.

García Sanjuán, L.; Díaz-Zorita Bonilla, M. 2013. Prácticas funerarias en estructuras negativas en el asentamiento prehistórico de Valencina de la Concepción (Sevilla): análisis contextual y osteoarqueológico. In García Sanjuán, L.; Vargas Jiménez, J. M.; Hurtado, V.; Ruiz Moreno, T.; Cruz-Auñón, R., ed – El asentamiento prehistórico de Valencina de la Concepción (Sevilla). Investigación y tutela en el 150 aniversario del descubrimiento de La Pastora. Sevilla: Universidad de Sevilla, p. 387-403.

García Sanjuán, L.; Murillo-Barroso, M. 2013. Social Complexity in Copper Age Southern Iberia (ca. 3200-2200 Cal B.C.). Reviewing the 'State' Hypothesis at Valencina de la Concepción (Seville, Spain). In Cruz Berrocal, M.; García Sanjuán, L.; Gilman, A., eds. – The Prehistory of Iberia: Debating Early Social Stratification and the State. New York: Routledge, p. 119-140.

García Sanjuán, L.; Vargas Jiménez, J. M.; Hurtado, V.; Ruiz Moreno, T.; Cruz-Auñón, R., ed – El asentamiento prehistórico de Valencina de la Concepción (Sevilla). Investigación y tutela en el 150 aniversario del descubrimiento de La Pastora. Sevilla: Universidad de Sevilla, 576 p.

Gonçalves, V. S. 1992. Revendo as Antas de Reguengos de Monsaraz. Lisboa: UNIARQ/INIC.

Hurtado, V. 1986. El Calcolítico en la cuenca media del Guadiana y la necrópolis de La Pijotilla. In Actas de la Mesa Redonda sobre Megalitismo Peninsular. Madrid: Ministerio de Cultura, p. 51-77.

Hurtado, V. 1999. Los inicios de la complejización social y el campaniforme en Extremadura. Spal. Seville. 8, p. 47-85.

Hurtado, V. 2008. Los recintos con fosos en la Cuenca Media del Guadiana. Era-Arqueologia. Lisbon. 8, p. 182-197.

Jorge, S. O. 1994. Colónias, fortificações, lugares monumentalizados. Trajectória das concepções sobre um tema do Calcolítico peninsular. Revista da Faculdade de Letras. Porto. II Serie XI, p. 447-546.

Lago, M.; Albergaria, J. 2001. O Cabeço do Torrão (Elvas): contextos e interpretaçoes previas de um lugar do Neolítico Alentejano. Era-Arqueologia. Lisbon. 4, p. 39-63.

Lago, M.; Duarte, C.; Valera, A. C.; Albergaria, J.; Almeida, F.; Carvalho, A. 1998. Povoado dos Perdigões (Reguengos de Mosaraz): dados preliminares dos trabalhos arqueológicos realizados em 1997. Revista portuguesa de Arqueologia. Lisbon. 1: 1, p. 45-152.

Lechuga, M.; Soto, M.; Rodríguez Ariza, M. O. 2014. El poblado calcolítico 'Venta del Rapa' (finales III milenio Cal. BC.), Mancha Real, Jaén. Un recinto de fosos entre las estribaciones de Sierra Mágina y el Alto Guadalquivir. Trabajos de Prehistoria. Madrid. 71: 2, p. 353-367.

Leisner, G.; Leisner, V. 1951. Antas do Concelho de Reguengos de Monsaraz. Lisboa: UNIARCH/INIC (1985).

Lizcano, R. 1999. El Polideportivo de Martos (Jaén): un yacimiento neolítico del IV milenio a.C. Nuevos datos para la reconstrucción del proceso histórico del Alto Guadalquivir. Córdoba: Obra Social y Cultural Cajasur, 333 p.

Lizcano, R., Camara, J. A., Riquelme, J. A., Cañabate, M. L., Sanchez, A.; Afonso, J. A. 1991-92. El Polideportivo de Martos. Producción económica y símbolos de cohesión en un asentamiento del Neolítico Final en las campiñas del Alto Guadalquivir. Cuadernos de Prehistoria de la Universidad de Granada. Granada. 16-17, p. 5-101.

MÁRQUEZ-ROMERO, J. E. 2003. Recintos Prehistóricos Atrincherados (RPA) en Andalucía (España): Una propuesta interpretativa. In Jorge, S. O. – Recintos murados da Pré-história recente. Técnicas constructivas e organização do espaço. Conservação, restauro e valorização patrimonial de arquitecturas pré-históricas. Porto: Faculdade de Letras da Universidade do Porto, p. 269-284.

MÁRQUEZ-ROMERO, J. E. 2006. Neolithic and Copper Age ditched enclosures and social inequality in the Iberian South (IV-III millennia cal BC). In Díaz-Del-Río, P.; García Sanjuán, L., eds – Social inequality in Iberian Late Prehistory. Oxford: BAR., p. 171-187. (BAR International Series; 1525).

MÁRQUEZ-ROMERO, J. E.; JIMÉNEZ-JÁIMEZ, V. 2010. Recintos de Fosos. Genealogía y significado de una tradición en la Prehistoria del suroeste de la Península Ibérica (IV-III milenios AC). Málaga: SPICUM Servicio de publicaciones de la Universidad de Málaga, 588 p.

MÁRQUEZ-ROMERO, J. E.; JIMÉNEZ-JÁIMEZ, V. 2013. Monumental ditched enclosures in Southern Iberia (fourth-third Millennia Cal BC). Antiquity. 87: 336, p. 447-460.

MÁRQUEZ-ROMERO, J. E.; JIMÉNEZ-JÁIMEZ, V. 2014. Recent Prehistory enclosures and funerary practices: some remarks. In Valera, A. C., ed – Recent Prehistoric Enclosures and Funerary Practices in Europe. Proceedings of the International Meeting held at the Gulbenkian Foundation (Lisbon, Portugal, November 2012). Oxford: BAR., p. 149-154. (Bar International Series; 2676).

MÁRQUEZ-ROMERO, J. E.; VALERA, A. C.; BECKER, H.; JIMÉNEZ-JÁIMEZ, V.; SUÁREZ PADILLA (2011. El Complexo Arqueológico dos Perdigões (Reguengos de Monsaraz, Portugal). Prospecciones Geofísicas – Campañas 2008-09. Trabajos de Prehistoria. Madrid. 68: 1, p. 175-186.

MARTÍN DE LA CRUZ, J. C.; LUCENA, A. 2003. Visiones y revisiones de Papa Uvas (Aljaraque, Huelva). In Jorge, S. O., ed – Recintos murados da Pré-história recente. Técnicas constructivas e organização do espaço. Conservação, restauro e valorização patrimonial de arquitecturas pré-históricas. Porto: Faculdade de Letras da Universidade do Porto, p. 285-306.

MARTÍN DE LA CRUZ, J. C. 1987. El Llanete de los Moros. Montoro, Córdoba, Excavaciones Arqueológicas en España, 151. Madrid: Ministerio de Cultura.

MOLINA, F.; CÁMARA, J. A.; CAPEL, J.; NÁJERA, T.; SÁEZ, L. 2004. Los Millares y la periodización de la Prehistoria del Sureste. In II-III Simposios de Prehistoria Cueva de Nerja. Nerja: Fundación Cueva de Nerja, p. 142-158.

MORÁN, E.; PARREIRA, R. 2003. O Povado calcolítico de Alcalar (Portimão) na paisagem cultural do Alvor no III milenio antes da nossa era. In Jorge, S. O. ed – Recintos murados da Pré-história recente. Técnicas constructivas e organização do espaço. Conservação, restauro e valorização patrimonial de arquitecturas pré-históricas. Porto: Faculdade de Letras da Universidade do Porto, p. 307-328.

NOCETE, F. 2001. Tercer milenio antes de nuestra era. Relaciones y contradicciones centro/periferia en el Valle del Guadalquivir. Barcelona: Bellaterra, 187 p.

RODRIGUES, F. 2014. Skeletons in the ditch: funerary activity in ditched enclosures of Porto Torrão (Ferreira do Alentejo, Beja). In Valera, A. C., ed – Recent Prehistoric Enclosures and Funerary Practices in Europe. Proceedings of the International Meeting held at the Gulbenkian Foundation (Lisbon, Portugal, November 2012). Oxford: BAR., p. 59-70. (Bar International Series; 2676).

VALERA, A. C. 2006. A margem esquerda do Guadiana (região de Mourão), dos finais do 4º aos inícios do 2º milénio AC. ERA-Arqueologia. Lisbon. 7, p. 136-210.

VALERA, A. C. 2012a. Mind the gap: Neolithic and Chalcolithic enclosures of South Portugal. In Gibson, A., ed – Enclosing the Neolithic. Recent studies in Britain and Europe. Oxford: BAR., p. 165-183. (BAR International Series; 2440).

VALERA, A. C. 2012b. Ditches, pits and hypogea: new data and new problems in South Portugal Late Neolithic and Chalcolithic practices. In Gibaja, J. F; Carvalho, A. F.; Chambon, P., ed. – Funerary Practices in the Iberian Peninsula from the Mesolithic to the Chalcolithic. Oxford: BAR., p. 103-112. (BAR International Series; 2417).

VALERA, A. C. 2013. Cronologia dos recintos de fossos da Pré-História Recente em território português. In Arnaud, J. M.; Martins, A.; Neves, C., ed – Arqueologia em Portugal: 150 Anos. Lisboa: Associação dos Arqueólogos Portugueses, p. 335-343.

Valera, A. C.; Becker, H.; Boaventura, R. 2013a. Moreiros 2 (Arronches, Portalegre): geofísica e cronologia dos recintos interiores. Apontamentos de Arqueologia e Património. Lisbon. 9, p. 37-46.

Valera, A. C.; Filipe, I. 2004. O povoado do Porto Torrão (Ferreira do Alentejo). ERA-Arqueologia. Lisbon. 6, p. 28-61.

Valera, A. C.; Filipe, V.; Cabaço, N. 2013b. O recinto de fosso de Outeiro Alto 2 (Brinches, Serpa). Apontamentos de Arqueologia e Património. Lisbon. 9, p. 21-35.

Valera, A. C.; Godinho, R. 2009. A gestão da norte nos Perdigões (Reguengos de Monsaraz). Novos dados, novos problemas. Estudos Arqueológicos de Oeiras. Lisbon. 17, p. 371-387.

Valera, A. C.; Santos, H.; Figueiredo, M.; Granja, R. (in press). Contextos funerários na periferia do Porto Torrão: Cardim 6 e Carrascal 2. In Actas do 4º Colóquio de Arqueologia do Alqueva, Beja (2010).

Valera, A. C.; Silva, A. M. 2011. Datações de radiocarbono para os Perdigões (1): contextos com restos humanos nos sectores I and Q. Apontamentos de Arqueologia e Património. Lisbon. 7, p. 7-14.

Valera, A. C.; Silva, A. M.; Márquez-Romero, J. M. 2014. The temporality of Perdigões enclosures: absolute chronology of the structures and social practices. Spal. Sevilla. 23, p. 11-26.

Vargas, J. M. 2004. Carta Arqueológica Municipal de Valencina de la Concepción. Sevilla: Junta de Andalucía.

Whittle, A.; Healy, F.; Bayliss, A. 2011. Gathering Time. Dating the Early Neolithic enclosures of Southern Britiain and Ireland. Oxford: Oxbow books.

Zafra, N.; Hornos, F.; Castro, M. 1999. Una macro-aldea en el origen del modo de vida campesino: Marroquíes Bajos (Jaén) c. 2500-2000 cal. ANE. Trabajos de Prehistoria. Madrid. 56: 1, p. 77-102.

Zafra, N.; Castro, M.; Hornos, F. 2003. Sucesión y simultaneidad en un gran asentamiento: la cronología de la macro-aldea de Marroquíes Bajos, Jaén. c. 2500-2000 cal ANE. Trabajos de Prehistoria. Madrid. 60: 2, p. 79-90.

Ditched enclosures and the ideologies of death in the Late Neolithic and Chalcolithic South Portugal

António Carlos VALERA

NIA-ERA Arqueologia, Interdisciplinary Center for Archaeology and Evolution of Human Behavior (ICArEHB), Cç. Santa Catarina 9C, 1495-705 Cruz Quebrada-Dafundo. Portugal
antoniovalera@era-arqueologia.pt

Abstract

South Portugal Recent Prehistory has been in permanent empirical 'revolution' since the beginning of this century, namely in what concerns funerary practices. The traditional image of the megalithic monuments as the main funerary architectures of Neolithic and Chalcolithic communities no longer stands. In the context of more diversified funerary architectures and spaces, some ditched enclosures have emerged as places that maintain specific special connections with areas of necropolis and revealing themselves as places where funerary practices and body manipulations appear as significant social practices. It is argued that the funerary world is part of a cosmogony embedded and expressed by some of those enclosures and by the inter-contextual relations they established.

Keywords: *Enclosures, funerary practices, Neolithic, South Portugal*

Résumé

La Préhistoire du sud du Portugal est en 'revolution' empirique permanente depuis le début du siècle, en particulier en ce concerne les pratiques funéraires. L'image traditionnelle des monuments mégalithiques comme seules architectures funéraires des périodes néolithiques et chalcolithiques est aujourd'hui dépassée. Dans un contexte de plus grande variété d'architectures et d'espaces funéraires, certaines enceintes fossoyées se sont révélées comme des lieux qui maintiennent des relations étroites avec les nécropoles et également comme des espaces où se déroulent des pratiques funéraires et des manipulations de corps, ce qui témoigne de pratiques sociales évidentes. Dans cet article, il est présenté l'hypothèse selon laquelle le monde funéraire est partie intégrante de la cosmogonie qui fonde ces enceintes and par les relations qu'elles entretiennent avec les autres contextes.

Mots-clés: *Enceinte, pratiques funéraires, Néolithique, Sud Portugal*

Introduction

The traditional literature on Portuguese Recent Prehistory always have established a dichotomy between settlements and places of economic activities grouped in one side and places of sacred and symbolic activities (including here the funerary practices and contexts) clustered in the other. This separated spatiality was assumed as a projection of clearly separable dimensions of life, as we can experience today, especially in the western world.

However, the projection in past societies of the modern western social clustering of existence has been criticized for long in all historical sciences. In the case of Portuguese Recent Prehistory, current data on enclosures is reinforcing this criticism, showing how apparently spatial separated dimensions of life and architecture are in fact structurally linked and sometimes fused to the point of creating problems to our set of conceptual tools.

Being a phenomenon of continental scale during Recent Prehistory, enclosures present a great variety of architectonic solutions, locations, sizes and contexts. That multiplicity has generated diversified interpretations: domestic settlements, places of refuge, corrals, places for exchange, communal assemblies, places of social aggregation and identity management, sacred places, locals for funerary practices, places related to astronomic observations, route markers, etc. (Andersen, 1997). Many of these functionalities may be combined in numerous of these contexts, where a cosmological dimension (places that express world views) is underlying that plurality of specific functions. This cosmological reference is present in astronomic orientations of many of these sites, in the places chosen for their locations and in the ways they organize meaningful large scale landscapes or in the frequency in which they reveal themselves as stages for social practices highly ritualized: ceremonial feasts for interchange, similar or not to Potlatch type ceremonies (Mauss, 2008), funerary practices, complex body manipulations and depositions of human and animal remains or particular observances in specific periods of the year that architecture seems to materialize. Summing up, many of these enclosures are impregnated with cosmological meaning, assuming a holistic significance that is resistant to modern social categorization. One of those resistances is precisely related to the idea of a clear separation of worlds between the living and the dead and to the assumption that the social practices involving the later are passive mirrors of the former.

The last two decades revealed the presence of ditched enclosure in South Portugal to an extent previously unsuspected (Valera, 2013a) (Figure 1). Radiocarbon is showing that they emerged in this area in the Late Neolithic (generally between 3350 to 2900 BC) and developed through the Chalcolithic (3rd millennium BC) (Figure 2). Recent unpublished dates bring the emergence of ditched enclosures to the late Middle Neolithic (3600-3500 BC) also in Alentejo region. Available data shows that since the beginning they show a strong articulation with the funerary contexts. This relation can be perceived in four main domains:
- they share cosmological ideas;
- they may be linked in the organization of landscapes and places;
- they may spatially structure each other.
- and they may be merged.

These relations, that functioned at different scales (from the site to the landscape) and different social dimensions (from the material practice to the ideological perception), talk about an ideological and ontological fluidity that generates contextual mixtures or, more adequately, contextual wholes.

1. Sharing cosmological ideas

Regarding cosmology, it has been noted that megalithic passage graves reveal the preoccupation with eastern orientations and with the Sun rising (Hoskins, 2009) or other stars, like the Aldebaran (Silva, 2010). This same general fact was also documented for megalithic cromlechs of South Portugal (Silva e Calado, 2003). A similar ideological prescription was recognized in both megalithic architectures that, serving different symbolic purposes, shared the same social space: the sacred and symbolic world.

The recent research in ditched enclosures in South Portugal shows that the same general fact can also be observed in many of these sites (Valera, 2013b), especially when complete plans are available (Figure 3).

At Perdigões, the inner Late Neolithic enclosure has its circularity interrupted by a strait layout of the south part of the ditch until the gate (Figure 3a). This axis is roughly aligned with the summer solstice at sunrise. The same circumstance can be observed in another ditch involving the previous, but dating from the Chalcolithic. From this same period, the gates of the double outside ditch system also seem to have astronomic orientations: the eastern ones are orientated to both solstices at sunrise and the western ones are orientated at both solstices at sunset.

This pattern of general orientation of gates to solstices and equinoxes (or to the moon larger standstill) is present in several other sites, like Xancra, Santa Vitória, Outeiro Alto 2 or Bela Vista 5 (Figure 3b to 3e) showing that a specific cosmological order is shared by enclosures and megalithic architectures. The same arguments can be presented to same walled enclosures, namely in Central-North Portugal.

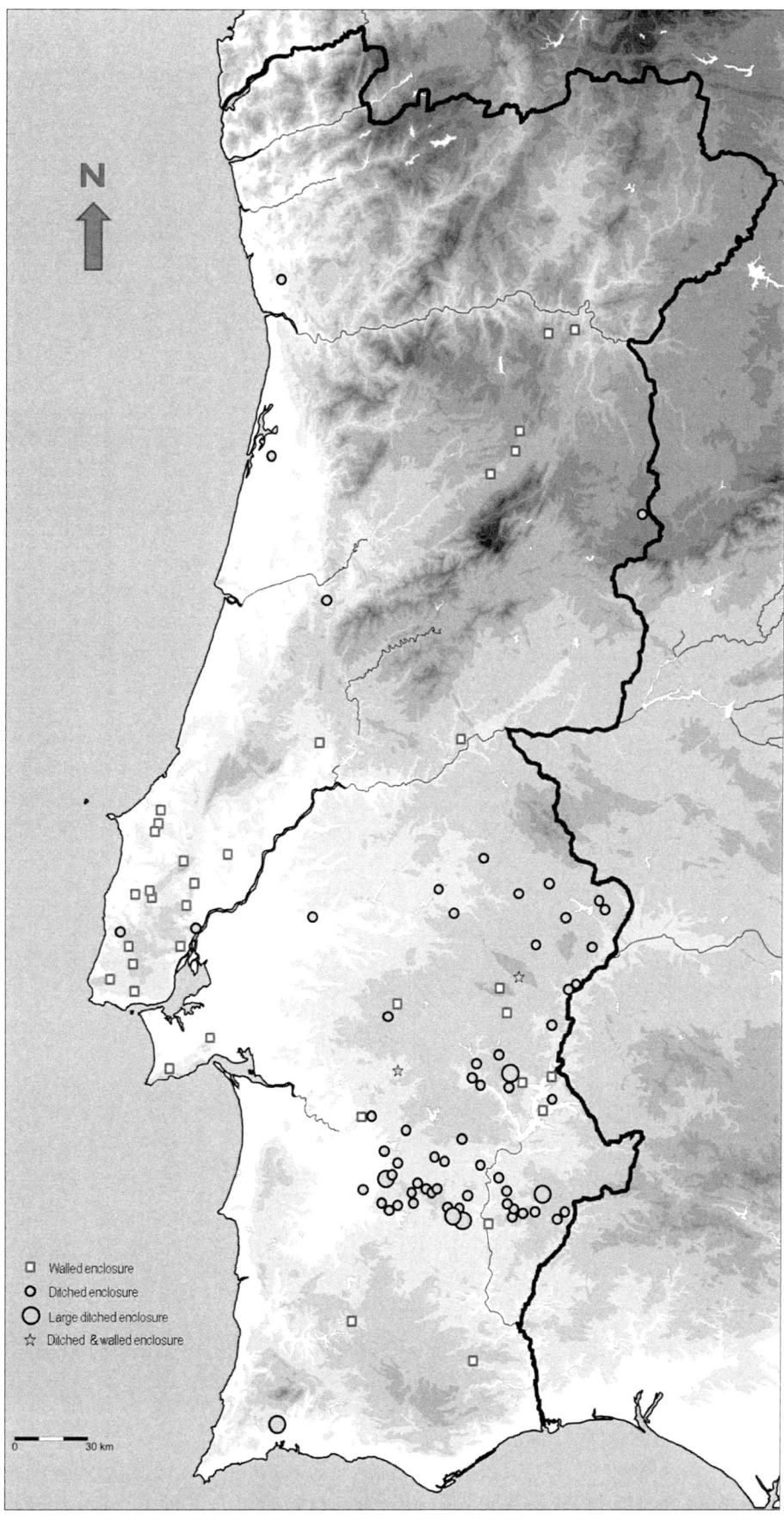

FIGURE 1. DISTRIBUTION OF ENCLOSURES IN PORTUGAL. SQUARES – WALLED ENCLOSURES; SMALL CIRCLES – DITCHED ENCLOSURES; LARGE CIRCLES – LARGE DITCHED ENCLOSURES; STARS – SITES WITH DITCHED AND WALLED ENCLOSURES.

Ref.	BP	Context
Beta-330092	4530±40	Pedrigões ditch 12
Beta-315242	4450±30	Perdigões ditch 6 base
Beta-318359	4390±30	Perdigões ditch 6 top
Beta-350352	4390±30	Perdigões ditch 5
Wk18487	4538±32	Juromenha 1
Wk18488	4547±35	Juromenha 1
Beta-169263	4540±100	Juromenha 1
Beta-169264	4550±40	Juromenha 1
OxA-5443	4540±60	S. Jorge de Ficalho
Beta-350350	4410±30	Moreiros 2
Beta-350351	4350±30	Moreiros 2
Wk-38618	4464±29	Monte da Contenda 1
Wk-38619	4478±29	Monte da Contenda 1
Sac-2232	4390±50	Porto Torrão Ditch 1
Oxa-5534	4010±70	Torre dos Exporão
Beta-285098	4050±40	Perdigões ditch 3
Beta-285096	4050±40	Perdigões ditch 3
Beta-285095	3980±40	Perdigões ditch 3
Beta-285097	3980±40	Perdigões ditch 4
Beta-289264	3940±40	Perdigões ditch 4
Beta-339604	3920±30	Outeiro Alto 2
Beta-315725	3890±30	Perdigões ditch 1
Beta-315723	3820±30	Perdigões ditch 1
Beta-315722	3890±30	Perdigões ditch 1
Beta-315721	3840±30	Perdigões ditch 1
Beta-315719	3780±30	Perdigões ditch 1
Beta-315720	3860±30	Perdigões ditch 1
Beta-315716	3770±30	Perdigões ditch 1
Sac-2027	3810±50	Porto Torrão ditch 2
Sac-2233	3910±80	Porto Torrão ditch 2
Sac-2028	3700±60	Porto Torrão ditch 2
Beta-261320	3770±40	Horta dos Albardões 3
Beta-324673	3810±30	Bela Vista 5 ditch 2
Beta-324674	3770±30	Bela Vista 5 ditch 1
Beta-324676	3650±30	Bela Vista 5 ditch 1

TABLE 1. RADIOCARBON DATES AVAILABLE FOR SOUTH PORTUGAL DITCHED ENCLOSURES. WITH THE EXCEPTION OF TORRE DO ESPORÃO, ONLY THE DATES SAMPLES FROM INSIDE THE DITCHES WERE CONSIDERED.

This general search for an eastern orientation is also visible in the locations selected to build the enclosures that are frequently positioned in topographies orientated to east. That is evident in Perdigões, where the enclosures were located in a natural theatre that has it visibility over the landscape limited to east and the limits of that visibility are roughly coincident with the solstices (Figure 4a), turning the horizon in a annual solar 'calendar' and where the hill of Monsaraz, located at 90°, marks the equinoxes (Valera, 2010a). In Xancra the enclosures are situated in the middle of a smooth slope, cut by two streams that are naturally convergent to a point with the same orientation of the enclosure's gates (winter solstice or moon larger standstill), showing a clear relation between the enclosures architecture, topography, the horizon and astronomic events. Similar circumstances can be observed in the megalithic cromlechs of the region, like Almendres, Portela dos Mogos, Vale d'el Rei or Vale Maria do Meio (Silva, Calado, 2003), underlying the ideological proximity between these constructions, that Perdigões and Torrão seem to physically materialize: in these two sites enclosures and cromlechs are side by side. Many other ditched enclosures show the same general settings in slopes or natural theatres, like Folha do Ouro, Paraíso, Monte do Olival, Bela Vista 5, Monte da Contenda, Charneca, Nobre 2 or Lobeira de Cima. Enclosures are, therefore, related to landscapes in ways that cannot be reduced to the strictly economic and political roles (resources management, territorial control).

2. Organization of landscapes and places

In fact, at least since the Late Neolithic, ditched enclosures and megalithic architectures participate in the building up of highly symbolic places and landscapes through topographic and architectonic choices that provide specific visual relations and through the formation of places of long term emblematic reference.

Perdigões is an emblematic example. As referred, the site was imbedded in a natural topographical theatre, open to east with the limits of the overture roughly coinciding with both solstices at sunrise. Between the enclosure and the horizon marked by the Monsaraz hill there was a large megalithic landscape with

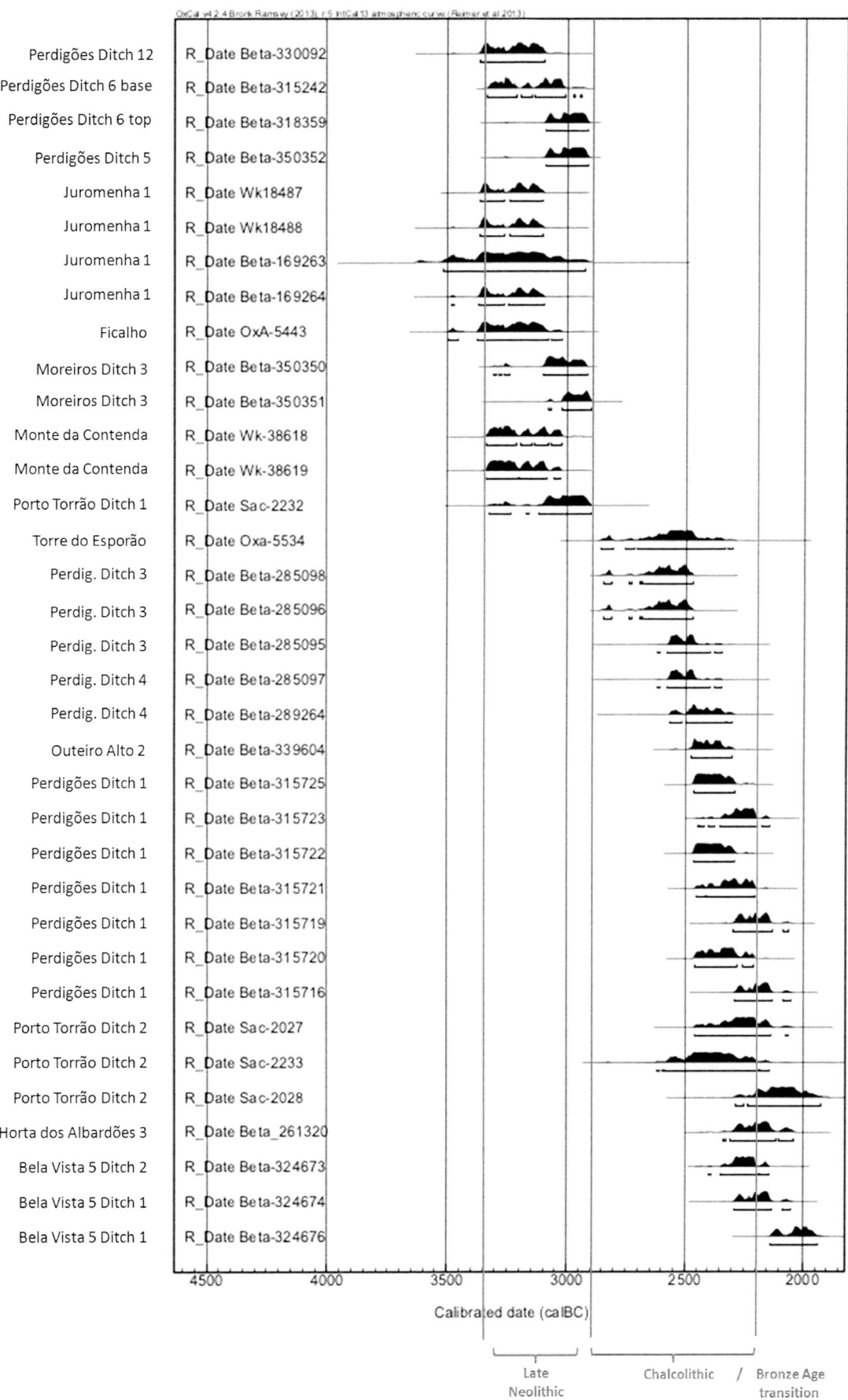

Figure 2. Radiocarbon dates available for South Portugal ditched enclosures (corresponding to 10 sites). With the exception of one site, only dates from inside ditches were considered.

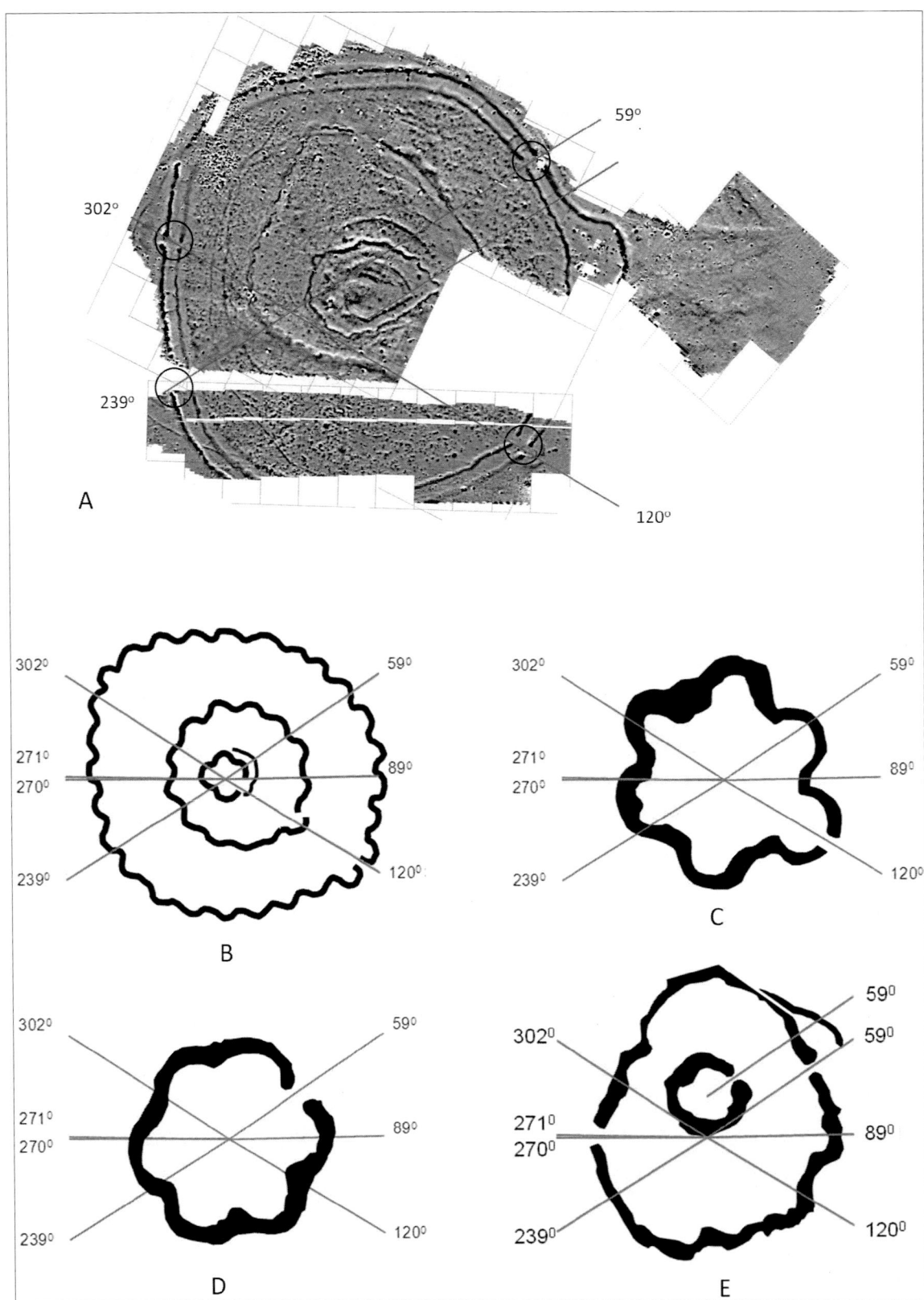

FIGURE 3. GATE ORIENTATIONS: A- PERDIGÕES; B- XANCRA; C- OUTEIRO ALTO 2; D- SANTA VITÓRIA; E- BELA VISTA 5.

more than a hundred passage graves and several standing stones and cromlechs (one of them just outside the enclosure, in the eastern side). A visual alignment between Perdigões, the areas of two biggest decorated standing stones of the region and the prominent hill of Monsaraz can also be detected (Figure 4). The enclosures, the megalithic monuments, their locations and visual connections, all participate in a construction of a highly symbolic local scenery: an interdependent meaningful landscape and not a dichotomised one, where past and new buildings and sites are integrated in the construction of a sense of particular order.

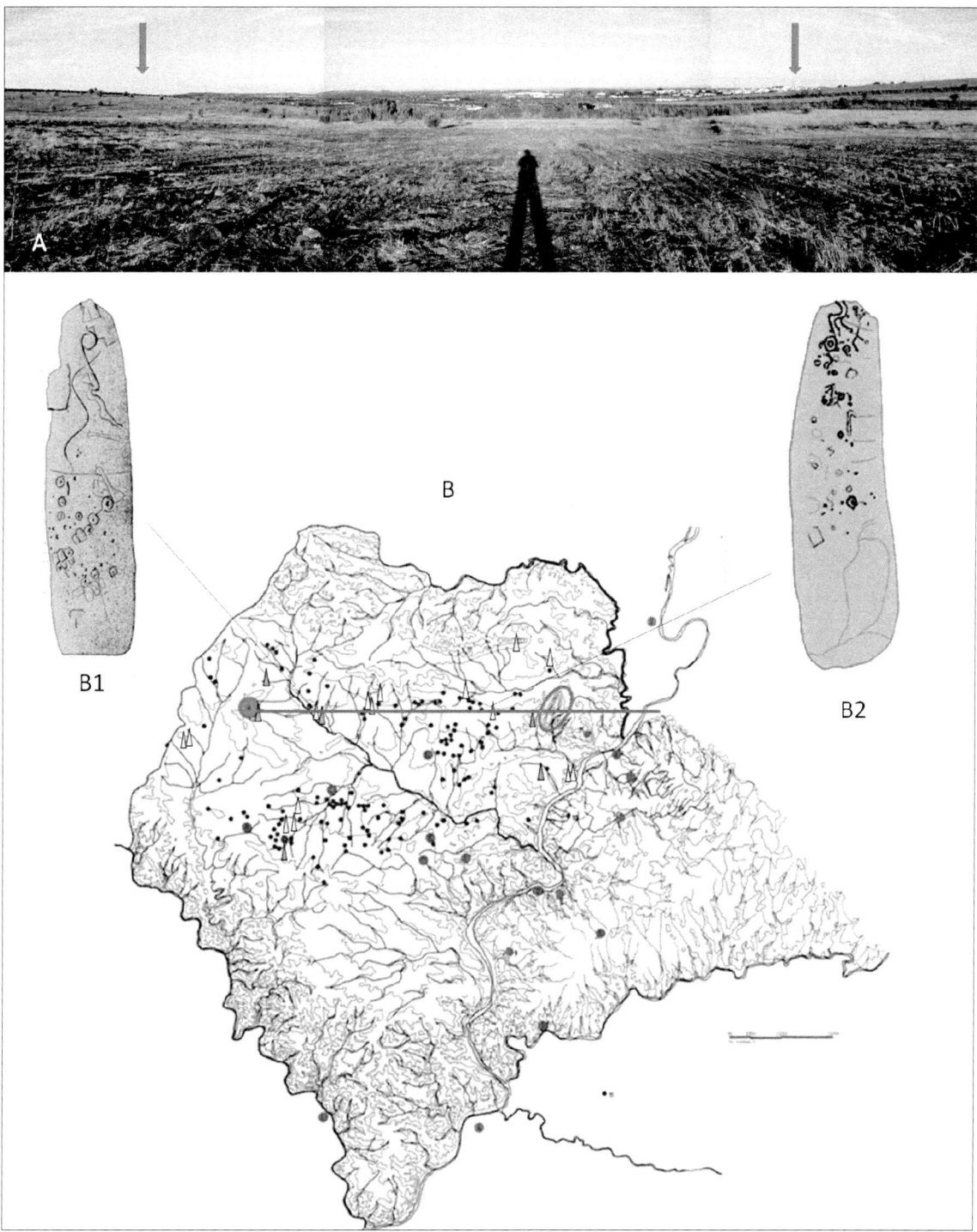

FIGURE 4. LANDSCAPE OF PERDIGÕES ENCLOSURE. A- EASTERN VISUAL HORIZON FROM INSIDE THE ENCLOSURE (ARROWS MARK THE SOLSTICES); B- EQUINOXES LINEAR CONNECTIONS BETWEEN PERDIGÕES, TWO DECORATED STANDING STONES AND THE HILL OF MONSARAZ.

At Outeiro Alto 2 (Figure 5) the relation between the enclosure and the funerary contexts is expressed in diachronic terms. The site is located in a small hill. In its north extremity a small timber circle was built, surrounded by three funerary hypogea and a funerary pit, dating from Late Neolithic (second

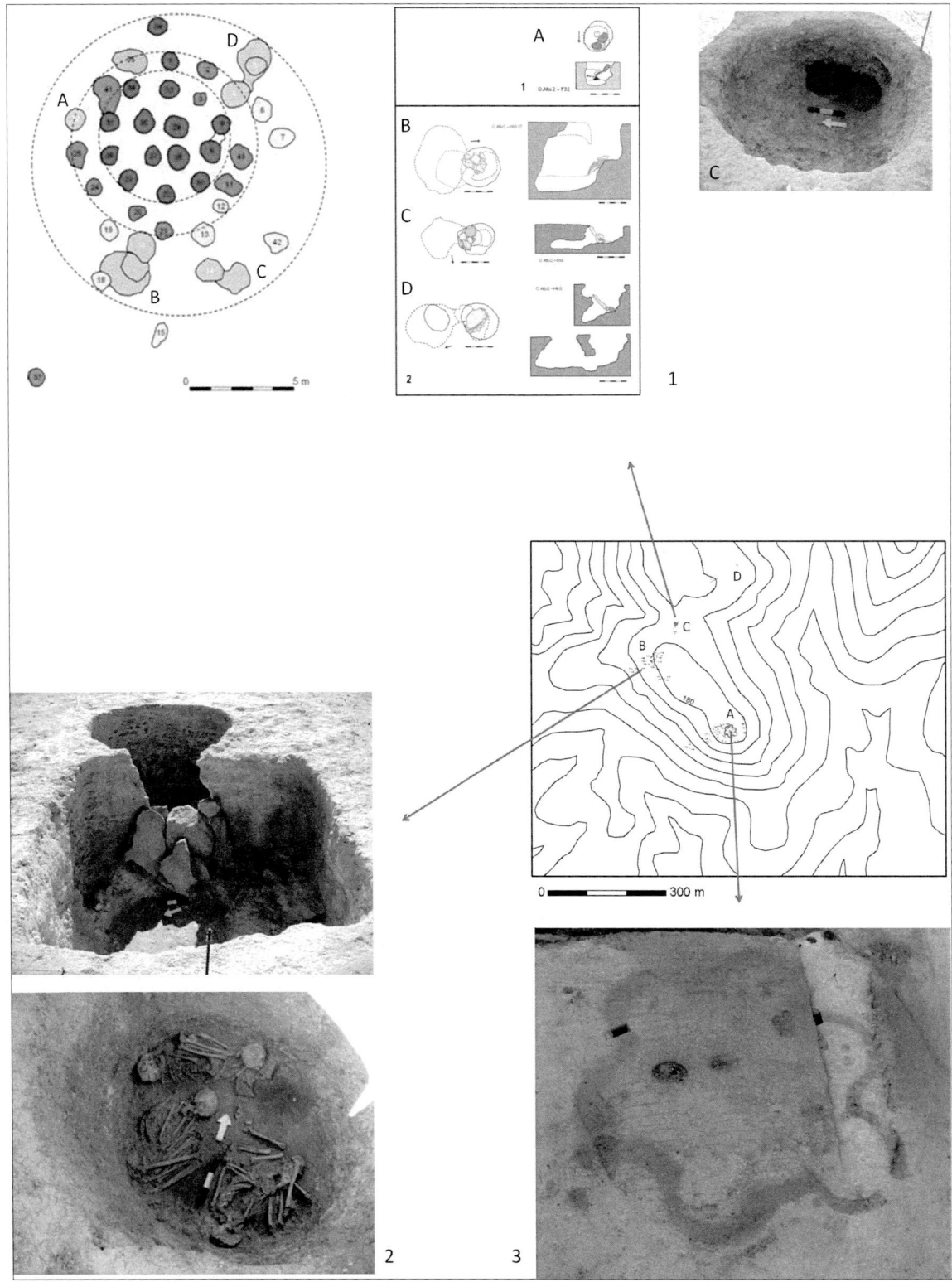

FIGURE 5. OUTEIRO ALTO 2: 1- LATE NEOLITHIC TIMBER CIRCLE AND NECROPOLIS; 2- BRONZE AGE NECROPOLIS; 3- CHALCOLITHIC DITCHED ENCLOSURE.

half of the 4th millennium BC). In the Late Chalcolithic an also small patterned sinuous ditched enclosure with the gate aligned to the winter solstice was built in the other extremity of the hill. Finally, in the Bronze Age (first half of the 2nd millennium BC), a necropolis of funerary pits and hypogea was added in the northeast part of the hill (Valera, Filipe, 2010). In the long term, but with significant intervals, a place of social and symbolic relevance was being built by the aggregation sequence of the enclosure and the funerary contexts. In fact, despite the clustered distribution of the different phases of occupation, what stands is the selection of the same hill where a set of ritualized constructions and practices connected to life and death seem to be the catalyser of the recurrent use of the same place.

A similar process, but shorter in time, may be seen in already mentioned site of Torrão, where in a small hill a Late Neolithic enclosure, a megalithic cromlech and a small megalithic tomb are associated (Lago, Albergaria, 2001): even if they were not built exactly in the same period, by the end of the 4th millennium BC they all participate in the construction of the meaning of the site.

3. Enclosures and necropolis areas

In some cases, during the 3rd millennium BC, contemporaneous enclosures and areas of necropolis are mutually structuring each other. This happens especially in the sites that grew to become large ditched enclosures with a capacity to aggregate (if continuously or periodically, is something still open to debate) a significant amount of people. In Perdigões, during the Chalcolithic, a necropolis with several *tholoi* type tombs was built at the eastern side of the enclosures (Figure 6a), between them and the previous megalithic cromlech (Valera *et al.* 2014). This group of collective tombs, apparently exclusively used for secondary depositions, was built precisely in the middle of the eastern opening of the natural theatre where the enclosures were located and where the slope gives way to the valley punctuated by megalithic passage graves. More than establishing a border, the necropolis provided a link through a visual (and walking) trajectory that connected the enclosures, the necropolis of *tholoi* type tombs, the cromlech, the megalithic landscape and the eastern horizon.

At Alcalar several clustered groups of funerary monuments surrounded the enclosure (Morán, 2008), here in the northern quadrant. At Porto Torrão, during the Chalcolithic, clusters of *tholoi* and hypogea are known in the South and Eastern limits of the site (Valera, 2010b) (Figure 6b). The eastern necropolis seems to be particularly large, with geophysics showing the presence of tens or even hundreds of tombs, clustered around segments of ditches that, in one excavated context, were functioning as atriums of access to underground graves. The absence of the global plans of the ditched enclosures of Alcalar and Porto Torrão, though, prevents an analysis similar to the one done for Perdigões enclosures and their relations with the necropolis and with the local landscape. However, data relating the presence of funerary practices and body manipulations inside the enclosures (more in Porto Torrão and just punctual in Alcalar, where the areas excavated are small) suggest a certain spatial ambiguity and that a clear demarcation of spaces might not be so clear. This same general perception was developed for the similar site of Valencina de la Concepción, in southwest Spain (Costa Camaré *et al.* 2010).

4. Enclosures, funerary practices and body manipulations

In fact, during the 3rd millennium BC funerary contexts and practices invaded some enclosures. Inside Porto Torrão (Figure 7) we have burials in pits and depositions of parts of human remains in anatomical connexion and some scattered human bones inside ditches (Rodrigues, 2014). Although the number of represented individuals is small when compared with the numbers provided by the excavated tombs in the periphery of the enclosure, it reveals not just the presence of funerary practices with primary depositions inside the enclosure, but also the manipulation of body parts and their deposition in contexts that suggest other ritualized practices involving the human and animal remains rather than just formal funerary ones.

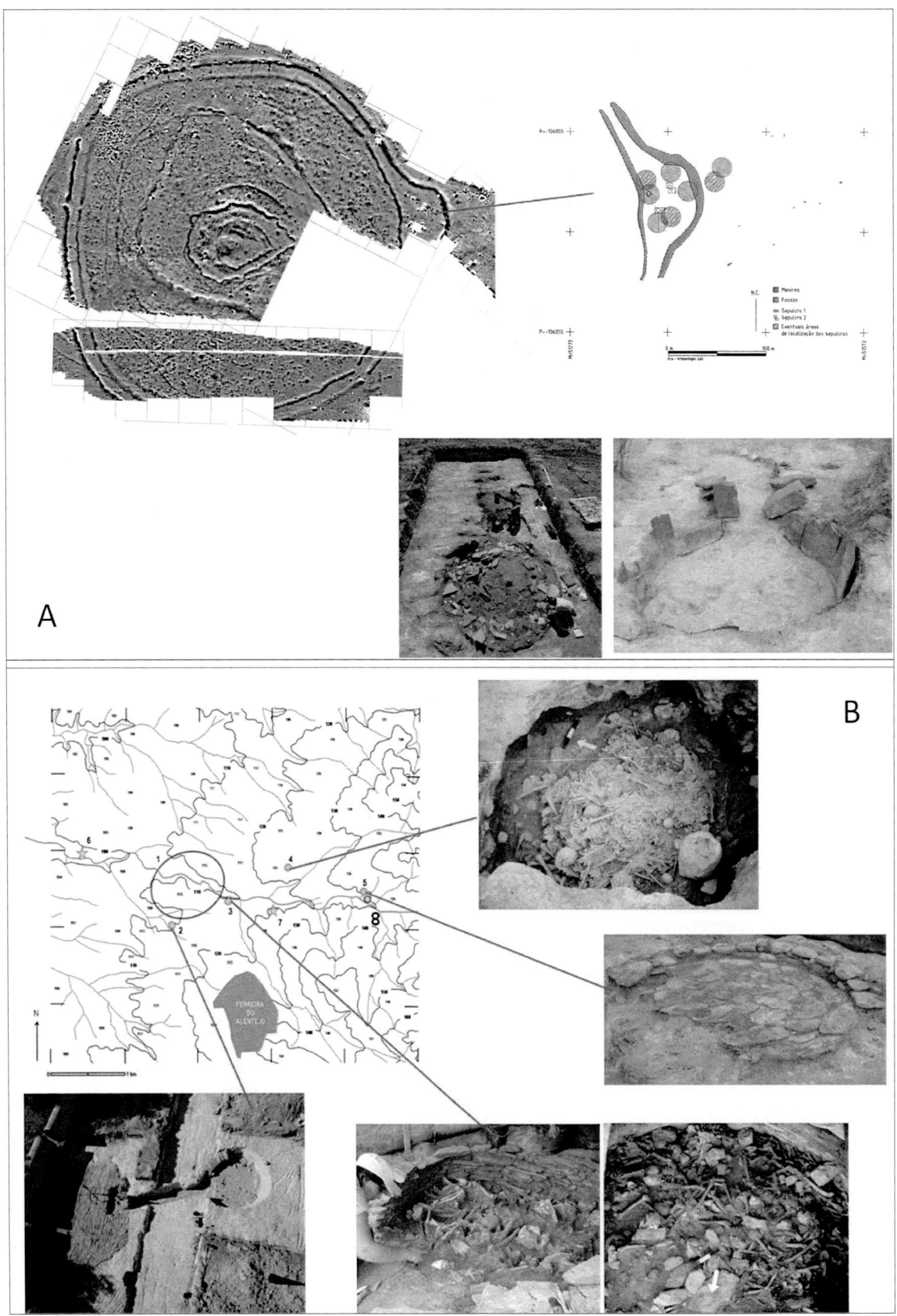

FIGURE 6. A- PERDIGÕES EASTERN NECROPOLIS; B- PORTO TORRÃO PERIPHERAL NECROPOLIS.

At Perdigões the presence of funerary practices and body manipulation inside the enclosure is more intense. By the middle 3rd millennium BC the outside ditch makes a curve to deliberately involve

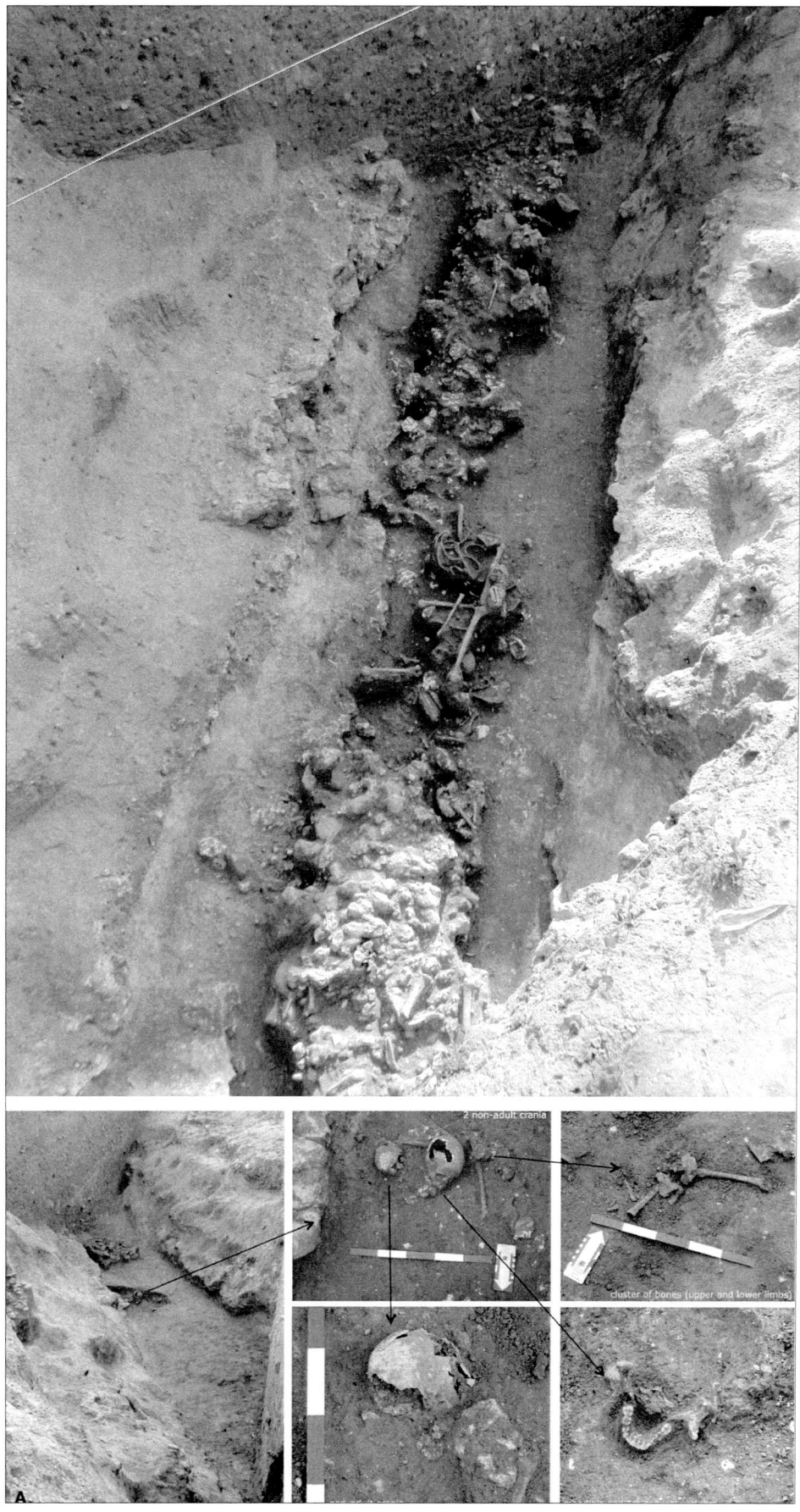

Figure 7. Porto Torrão ditch with depositions of human remains (after Rodrigues, 2014).

part of the previous *tholoi* necropolis while the tombs were still in use (Figure 6a), transforming an external funerary area in an internal one. At the same time human remains, along with animal remains, stones and pottery sherds, were being deposited inside ditches and, in the central area of the enclosures, secondary depositions of cremated remains of hundreds of individuals were being deposited in pits and in open area, sometimes mixed with parts of non cremated bodies still in anatomical connection (Valera *et al.*, 2014). Here, the minimum number of individuals represented inside the enclosures is of several hundreds.

Finally, at Bela Vista 5, in the last quarter of the 3rd millennium BC, the role of an enclosure as a stage for funerary practices reaches its more formal expression, as the enclosure might have been

FIGURE 8. BELA VISTA 5 ENCLOSURE, WITH CENTRAL PIT BURIAL OF A WOMAN.

built to receive the burial of a woman and associated practices (Valera, 2014): the burial was made in a central pit, the only structure inside the small inner ditched enclosure, surrounded by a larger one, built not as a continuous ditch but through the addition of segments with different sizes filled in different times with deposits of selected materials, mainly pottery sherds (Figure 8).

Although the number of enclosures with human remains inside is still relatively low (the large enclosure of Salvada also provided a human bone in surface prospection, suggesting the existence of similar contexts inside the perimeter of the ditches – Valera and Pereiro, in press), the available evidence for the Late Neolithic and Chalcolithic and the theoretical debate that is being generated clearly drift us from that old and strict dichotomy assumed for Alentejo region (and others) of settlements as a profane ground versus necropolis as a sacred ground, from the image of megalithic and cave graves as the exclusive spaces for the deceased, from the idea that human body manipulations were confined to funerary rituals of a more formal nature and, in sum, from the idea of a highly compartmented world.

Discussion

Prehistoric architectures, particularly the ones related with settlements, are frequently reduced to their more technical and functional dimensions and the relations established with landscapes reduced to resource exploitation and visual control of territories and circulation routes. However, while organizer of space, architecture simultaneously creates and traduces ways of conceiving the world, of experiencing and communicating it. As all throughout Europe, many of the Portuguese ditched enclosures, namely the ones for which we have complete plans, suggest that there is a strong cosmological meaning underlying their architecture, the landscape they help to structure and some of the social practices that were carried on inside them. They are 'places in relation', that organize as well as express a certain way of being in the world, not always ease to capture and define. In them we can find, fused, several of the dimensions in which our analytic modern spirit divides and categorizes the whole human social. In a way, they are holistic expressions of the communities that built and used them, for they 'seem to involve every dimension of the Neolithic existence of their times in one way or another, and their power and renown must have rested in part in this concentration of concerns' (Whittle, 2014: 7). Being so, the approaches to enclosures must not isolate them from the relations in which they are inserted and that gave them sense. It is not possible to understand a site like Perdigões disconnected from the megalithic landscape that is in front of it, visually captured between its topographical location and the provided 'solar horizon'. Perdigões 'are in relation' with a landscape inhabited by the living and by the dead (as the enclosure) and only in that relation the site can be understood.

In South Portugal, since they appeared (in the second half of the 4th millennium BC according to current available chronology), ditched enclosures reveal strong relations to principles that we can also detect in megalithic monuments and during the 3rd millennium the associations with funerary practices and body manipulations became more evident. Presently, social practices involving the treatment conceded to the dead and their body remains in the region during the 3rd millennium BC is characterized by a considerable diversity that is in clear contradiction with the perception of a certain homogeneity and spatial segregation traditionally induced by megalithic monuments.

As we have seen, the relation that we can appreciate between enclosures and the places and practices involving the dead may be perceived in different scales and dimensions, from the structuring of a place to a landscape organization, through a more apparent spatial demarcation or a more ambiguous one. The particular articulation between enclosures and funerary megalithic structures has been noted for other European regions (Evans, 1988a and 1988b; Whittle, 1988a and 1988b; Andersen, 2002; Bradley, 2005). It is not just a question of spatial proximity or of playing an aggregation role for the communities that built and used megalithic monuments (Edmonds, 1993 e 1999; Thomas, 1996; Marquez Romero, 2001), but a question of effective interpenetration of practices and of their spatial arrangements. Related in diverse ways and social dimensions, they helped to build a space that reflects what might be called a Neolithic cosmogony, a world view organized through diversified but coherent architectures and perpetuated through social practices, not clearly bounded and with a strong capacity for communal aggregation.

As to the contexts with human remains inside ditched enclosures, they cannot be understood exclusively *per se*, outside relations that may have been established between them or established with other social practices that also were occurring in those enclosures. It has been suggested that some of the distinct funerary practices and body manipulations that were occurring in large ditched enclosures may have been related as specific steps of ritualized procedures (Valera, Godinho, 2009). Enclosures, nearby tombs, ritualized practices of structured depositions of a variety of materials (where human bones are included) may be in some way connected in a sequential practice. A critical aware of that possibility must be developed, for we may be creating autonomous entities that make it difficult to understand the relational organization of the whole. As Whittle put it regarding the enclosures with human depositions 'Can we really distinguish between burial sites and sites with burials? (...) it is unwise to separate the human burials from the complex as a whole (...) The site is demonstrably the scene for prolonged depositions of various kinds, amongst which the human burials are only one element.' (Whittle, 1988b: 144-145). The argument is that they cannot be understood as an independent ritual procedure because their symbolic expression and social, spatial and temporal roles go far behind the need to provide a destiny to the dead.

These contextual mixtures show that dimensions of social live were more fluid and that we must approach territoriality in the bases of that fluidity. The diversity of funerary practices and contexts where bodies are manipulated during the Chalcolithic show that these actions were a central aspect of life that has no clear boundaries. Therefore, where aprioristic dichotomist perceptions of contexts established the framework for the interpretation of enclosures and of human remains and associated social practices we should now put the effort of looking for the part played by these contexts and practices in the construction of the contextual meaning and social role of a particular place or landscape.

In fact, the development of Neolithic (in a broader sense, integrating the Chalcolithic) may be considered a transitional period between more fluid perceptions of the world to more demarcated ones. Hybridism and ambiguity characterize these moments of cosmological and ontological transition and conformed human relations and human organizations of the world. We may consider that the dichotomy of domestic / non domestic regarding the organization of space and social dimensions of life is as much arguable (Bradley, 2003; 2005) as it is regarding the relations of humans and animals. For these relations levels of ontological fluidity have been assumed (Ingold, 1994, 2000; Valera, 2012), based in idea of more permeable ontological boundaries and in the concepts of dividual personhood (Hallowell, 1960; Marriott, 1976; Bird-David, 1999; Fowler, 2004). The perception of a dividual existence generates porous categories and a more relational connection between things and beings and between wholes and parts. It should be expected that this more permeable forms of organizing the world would be inserted in the ways human communities organized themselves in space and in time and that they would be expressed through a contextual fluidity and ambiguity regarding the spatial materialization of categories such as life and dead or sacred and profane. A situation of permeability of cosmological and ontological borders generates a situation of permeability of their materializations in space and in the architectonic forms of organizing it, creating problems to concepts such as domestic, sacred, necropolis, monument etc. due to their characteristics of exclusivity and of partition. As Thomas argued, 'By failing to recognize that the human lives exceed our conceptual schemes, we do not learn from the past so much as organise it. Most critically, where we seek to nullify the difference of the past by identifying people who are 'just like us' (...) we transform that difference to a universal sameness.' (Thomas, 2004: 238).

The relation between prehistoric ditched enclosures and the ideologies of death confront us with a historical situation that is quite different from ours and that demands the critical control of the conceptual tools we use to approach it. A control that must not be confused with any kind of naive idea of putting ourselves between brackets, for we can only talk about History as historical beings (Gadamer, 1998).

Bibliography

ANDERSEN, N. H. 1997. *The Sarup Enclosures. The Funnel Beaker Culture of the Sarup site including two causewayed camps compared to the contemporary settlements in the area and other European enclosures*. Aarhus: Jysk arkaeologisk Selskab, 404 p. (Jutland Archaeological Society Publications; 33.1.).

Andersen, N.H. 2002. Neolithic Enclosures of Scandinavia. In Varndell, G.; Topping P., eds. – *Enclosures in Neolithic Europe: Essays on Causewayed and Non-Causewayed Sites*. Oxford: Oxbow Books, p. 1-10.

BRADLEY, R. 2003. Life less ordinary: the ritualization of the domestic sphere in Later Prehistoric Europe. *Cambridge Archaeological Journal*. 13: 1, p. 5-23.

BRADLEY, R. 2005. *Ritual and domestic life in Prehistoric Europe*. London: Routledge, 234 p.

BIRD-DAVID, N. 1999) – 'Animism' revisited: Personhood, Environment, and Relational Epistemology. Current Anthropology. 40(1), p. S67-S91. (Special Issue Culture – A second chance ?).

EDMONDS, M. 1993. Interpreting causewayed enclosures in the past and the present. In Tilley, C., ed. – Interpretative archaeology. Oxford: Berg, p. 99-142.

EDMONDS, M. 1999. Ancestral Geographies of the Neolithic: landscapes, monuments and memory. London: Routledge, 173 p.

EVANS, C. 1988a. Monuments and analogy: the interpretation of causewayed enclosures. In Burgess, C.; Topping, P.; Mordant, C., Maddison, M., eds. – Enclosures and defences in the Neolithic of Western Europe, Oxford: Archaeopress, p. 47-73. (BAR International Series; 403 i).

EVANS, C. 1988b. Excavations at Haddenham, Cambridgeshire: a planned enclosure and its regional affinities. In Burgess, C.; Topping, P.; Mordant, C., Maddison, M., eds. – Enclosures and defences in the Neolithic of Western Europe, Oxford: Archaeopress, p. 127-148. (BAR International Series; 403 i).

FOWLER, C. 2004. The Archaeology of Personhood. An Anthropological Approach. London: Routledge, 184 p.

GADAMER, G. 1998. O problema da consciência histórica. V. N. de Gaia: Estratégias Criativas, 116 p.

HALLOWELL, A. I. 1960. Ojibwa ontology, behaviour, and world view. In Diamond., F., ed. – Culture in History: Essays in Honor of Paul Radin. New York: Columbia University Press, p. 17-49.

HOSKIN, M. 2009. Orientations of dolmens of Western Europe. In Cerdeño Serrano, M. L.; Rodríguez Caderot, G., eds. – Arqueoastronomía, Complutum, 20: 2. Madrid: UCM, p. 165-175.

INGOLD, T. 1994. From trust to domination. An alternative history of human-animal relations. In Manning, A.; Serpell, J., eds. – Animals and human society: Changing perspectives. London: Routledge, p. 1-22.

INGOLD, T. 2000. The Perception of the Environment. Essays on Livehood, Dwelling and Skill. London: Routledge, 480 p.

LAGO, M.; ALBERGARIA, J. 2001. O Cabeço do Torrão (Elvas): contextos e interpretações prévias de um lugar do Neolítico alentejano. Era Arqueologia. 4. Lisboa: Era Arqueologia / Colibri, p. 39-62.

MÁRQUEZ ROMERO, J. E. 2001. De los 'Campos de Silos' a los 'Agujeros Noegros': sobre pozos, depósitos y zanjas en la Prehistoria Reciente del Sur de la Península Ibérica. SPAL. 10, p. 207-220.

MARRIOT, M. 1976. Hindu transactions: diversity without dualism. In Kapferer, B., ed. – Transaction and Meaning: Directions in the Anthropology of exchange and symbolic behavior. Philadelphia: Institute for the Study of Human Issues, p. 109-142.

MORÁN, E. 2008. Organização espacial do Povoado Calcolítico de Alcalar (Algarve, Portugal). ERA Arqueologia. 8. Lisboa: Era Arqueologia / Colibri, p. 138-147.

MAUSS, M. 2008. Ensaio sobre a dádiva, Lisboa: Edições 70.

Rodrigues, F. 2014. Skeletons in the ditch: funerary activity in ditched enclosures of Porto Torrão (Ferreira do Alentejo, Beja)'. In Valera, A. C., ed. – Recent Prehistory enclosures and funerary practices. Oxford: Archaeopress, p. 59-69. (BAR. International Series; 2676).

Silva, C. M.; Calado, M. 2003. New astronomically significant directions of megalithic monuments in the Central Alentejo. Journal of Iberian Archaeology, 5. Porto: ADECAP, p. 67-88.

Silva, F. 2010. A new survey of Neolithic dolmens in central Portugal. Journal of Cosmology. 9, pp. 3094-3106.

Thomas, J. 1996. Time, Culture and Identity. An interpretive archaeology. London: Routledge, 288 p.

Thomas, J. 2004. Archaeology and modernity. London: Routledge, 275 p.

Valera, A. C. 2010a. Mapping the cosmos: a cognitive approach to iberian prehistoric enclosures. In Valera, A. C.; Evangelista, L., eds. – The idea of enclosure in recent iberian Prehistory, Oxford: Archaeopress, p. 99-108. (BAR International Series; 2124).

Valera, A. C. 2010b. Gestão da morte no 3º milénio AC no Porto Torrão (Ferreira do Alentejo): um primeiro contributo para a sua espacialidade. Apontamentos de Arqueologia e Património. 5, Lisboa: NIA-ERA Arqueologia, p. 57-62.

Valera, A. C. 2012. A 'Vaca de Almada' e o problema das relações Homem/Animal na Pré-História Recente. Almadan. 17. Almada: Centro de Arqueologia da Almada, p. 22-29.

Valera, A.C. 2013. Recintos de fossos da Pré-História Recente em Portugal. Investigação, discursos, salvaguarda e divulgação. Almadan. Segunda Série. 18, p. 93-110.

Valera, A. C. 2013b. Breve apontamento sobre a dimensão cosmogónica dos recintos de fossos da Pré-História Recente no Interior Alentejano., Cadernos do Endovélico. 1. Colibri/CMA, p. 51-63.

Valera, A. C., ed. 2014. Bela Vista 5. Um recinto do Final do 3º milénio a.n.e. (Mombeja, Beja), Era Monográfica. 2. Lisboa: Nia-Era.

Valera, A. C.; Filipe, V. 2010. Outeiro Alto 2 (Brinches, Serpa): nota preliminar sobre um espaço funerário e de socialização do Neolítico Final à Idade do Bronze. Apontamentos de Arqueologia e Património. 5. Lisboa: NIA-ERA Arqueologia, p. 49-56.

Valera, A. C.; Godinho, R. 2009. A gestão da morte nos Perdigões (Reguengos de Monsaraz): novos dados, novos problemas. Estudos Arqueológicos de Oeiras. 17. Oeiras: Câmara Municipal, p. 371-387.

Valera, A. C.; Silva, A. M.; Cunha, C.; Evangelista, L. S. 2014. Funerary practices and body manipulations at Neolithic and Chalcolithic Perdigões ditched enclosures (South Portugal). In Valera, A. C., ed. – Recent Prehistoric Enclosures and Funerary Practices. Oxford: Archaeopress, pp. 37-57. (BAR International Series; 2676).

Valera, A. C.; Pereiro, T. (in press). Os recintos de fossos da Salvada e Monte das Cabeceiras 2 (Beja, Portugal). Actas do VII Encontro de Arqueologia del Sudeste Peninsular. Aroche, pp. 17-27.

Whittle, A. 1988a. Contexts, activities, events – aspects of neolithic and copper age enclosures in central and western Europe, In Burgess C.; Topping P.; Mordant C.; Maddison M., eds. – Enclosures and defences in the Neolithic of Western Europe, Oxford: Archaeopress, pp. 1-19. (BAR International Series; 403 i).

Whittle, A. 1988b. Problems in Neolithic archaeology. Cambridge: Crambridge University Press (New Studies in Archaeology), 256 p.

Whittle, A. 2014. The times and timings of enclosures. In Valera, A. C., ed. – Recent Prehistoric Enclosures and Funerary Practices. Oxford: Archaeopress, pp. 1-12. (BAR International Series; 2676).

Towards a definition of the prehistoric landscape in the Plateau of *Sigarra*: visibility and territoriality between the Middle Neolithic and Bronze Age

Natalia SALAZAR ORTIZ
Universitat de Lleida, Departament d'Història Grup de Recerca en Arqueologia, Prehistòria i Història Antiga (GRAPHA), Plaça Víctor Siurana 1, 25003 Lleida. Spain
natalia.salazar@historia.udl.cat

Abstract

This study presents the practical application of GIS method of Cumulative Viewshwd Analysis in order to infer intervisibility relationships between archaeological sites of the Middle Neolithic, Chalcolithic and Bronze Age. We may found these sites chronologically and typologically connected in a particular historical territory structured around the ancient Iberian settlement and afterwards Roman town of Sigarra, in the geographic centre of the current Catalonia (els Prats de Rei, Barcelona). The Neolithic visibility patterns will show a lack of political and territorial hierarchy; while in the Bronze Age, in direct relation to the social complexity detected by archaeology, visibility patterns reflect a rich spatial organisation.

Keywords: Cumulative Viewshed Analysis, *visibility network, megalith tombs, Neolithic-Bronze Age, territory,* Sigarra

Résumé

Cette étude présente l'application pratique de la méthode de SIG Cumulative Viewshed Analysis, *afin de déduire les relations d'intervisibilité entre des sites archéologiques du Néolithique moyen, du Chalcolithique et de l'âge du Bronze. On observe que ces sites sont chronologiquement et typologiquement connectés dans un territoire historique particulier structuré autour de l'ancienne fortification ibérique et plus tard* municipium romain de Sigarra, *dans le centre géographique de l'actuel Catalogne (els Prats de Rei, Barcelone). Les modèles de visibilité pour l'époque néolithique montrent l'absence de hiérarchie politique et territoriale; tandis qu'à l'âge du Bronze, en accord avec la complexité sociale observée par les données archéologiques, les modèles de visibilité reflètent une organisation spatiale assez complexe.*

Mots-clés: Cumulative Viewshed Analysis, *réseau de visibilité, mégalithe, Néolithique/âge du Bronze, territoire,* Sigarra

Introduction

Visibility can be one of the keys that provide the answer to why a site is occupying a given location and not another. We can also consider the visual characteristics of a site by its position within the surrounding landscape, showing a visual relationship with other contemporary or earlier sites or with the natural components that integrate the landscape (Wheatley and Gillings 2002: 202).

The concept of visibility can be summarized as the quality and the distance that enable humans to recognize an object. Visibility itself can not be studied as a material object, but is the result of established relationship with the environment. It is not pottery, not a sculpture, nor a burial mound. Instead, its connection to the cultural context and the actors of the society is a fact (Zamora 2008). In a landscape, the location of an ancient burial mound would set up several questions: its situation is it casual, in the context in which it was located it was visible?, is it produced a particular emotional effect?, etc.

In this sense, the so-called post-processual archaeology gives meaning and an active part to the landscape as a set of elements that act as signs, symbols and messages interacting with society as a

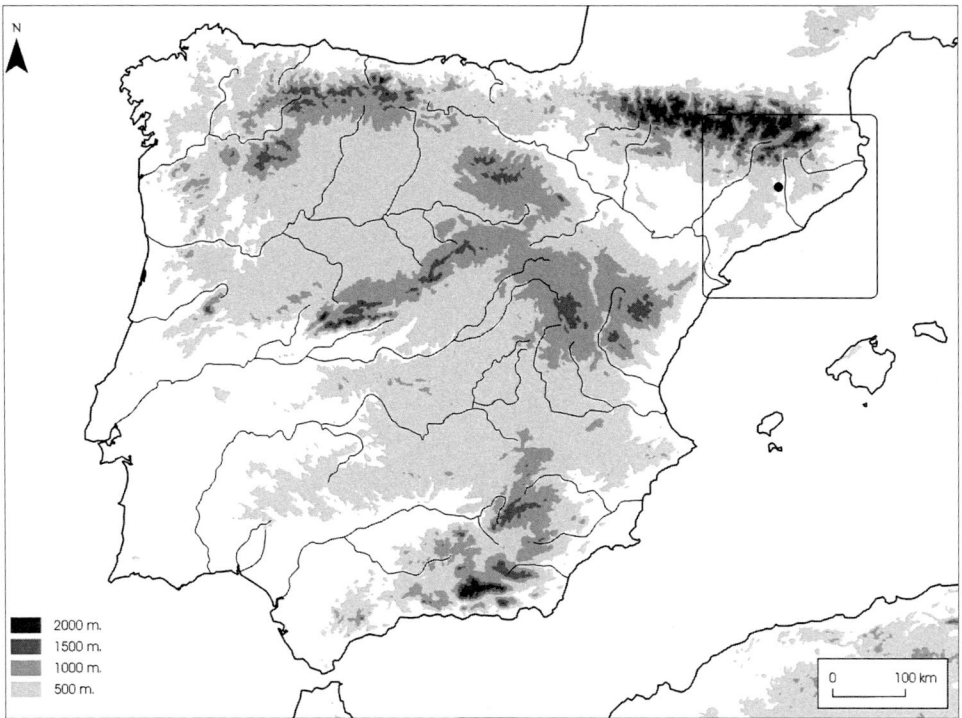

FIGURE 1. LOCATION OF THE PLATEAU OF *SIGARRA* ON THE IBERIAN PENINSULA MAP.

whole, in its parts and with the individual (García 2005: 244). It is within this space where visibility has an important role, since it is the sensory transmitter of these signs and symbols between social components within the landscape.

In summary visibility can be a useful tool for analyzing a landscape from a practical point of view (control of the territory and defence of settlements) or from a symbolic perspective (e.g., visibility of the anthropic elements and / or artistic, religious or funeral ones). Thus, we can differentiate between quantitative methods for studying spatial aspects of a visual event (processual perspective) and the phenomenological analysis of the visible elements in the landscape (post-processual perspective).

From both perspectives we analyze and calculate visibility relationships that may exist between a number of archaeological sites dating from the Middle Neolithic and Bronze Age. Our ultimate goal is to try to define and compare the probable existence of a territorial structure within the communities of these periods documented in the landscape dominated by the Iberian settlement, later Roman town, of *Sigarra*, in the geographic centre of the current Catalunya (els Prats de Rei, Barcelona, Fig. 1) (Salazar 2012).

1. Visibility analysis GIS methods

Visibility can be calculated and analyzed by GIS using different tools. The functions most used in the calculation of visibility let you know the surface area viewable from a certain observation point, visual connections between different locations and identify as well, territorial or settlement units.

1.1. Line of sight (LOS)

GIS provide a tool for incorporating visibility in the archaeological analysis that allows the calculation of simple viewshed of a point by determining which parts of the study area theoretically seen from a given observation location, and allowing subsequent determination of direct intervisibility between a set of elements.

That is, given two locations we can calculate the line of sight (LOS) between them: the straight line that is not truncated by the topography of the area allowing, therefore, direct visual communication between the two landmarks.

The calculation of a line of sight or viewshed of a place is based on a raster map and is currently available as own functionality in many GIS. To calculate a viewshed is necessary to have the following thematic layers of information: A Digital Elevation Model (DEM) and a layer that encodes the location or locations from which you want to determine the viewshed. In our study these locations will be mapped as points that represent each a site.

The calculation routine described requires drawing a straight line from each point of origin to all other raster cells of the elevation model. In this way you can get the heights of all the cells that lie along the straight line from the origin to the destination cells, to determine whether or not they exceed the height of the line in three dimensions.

The achieved result can be either positive or negative, conventionally encoded as a 1 for a visible cell or 0 to a cell which is not visible. If this calculation for the entire raster is implemented, the result is a binary image with the areas of the landscape that have a direct line of sight to the target cell, coded 1, and those with no line of sight commonly encoded with 0. We will refer to the new image as viewshed map or map of visibility.

Many GIS allows restrictions to visibility calculations, such as limiting the extent of the grid cells to analyze or also considering the viewing angle. Most GIS specification also allows assigning to the observer a height above the DEM surface. For an adult human often a standard height of 1.7 m is used, even though the human eye height above the ground rather depend on the particular subject. If we analyze the viewshed of a structure such as a watchtower we should take into account the height of the observation platform (Cazorla 2008).

In our case, since we deal mostly with sites composed by underground structures excavated and / or still buried in the ground, we will consider the altitude above sea level of each site, without adding any other parameter.

Viewshed should be the starting point for any further operations and it determines all existing lines of vision 360 degrees around the point of observation. So we should found whether the LOS from the observation point to each raster cell is or not interrupted by the topography of the land. As a result we will obtain a binary map where each cell responds to the result of a LOS taken from an observation point (Wheatley and Gillings 2002: 181-184).

1.2. Measuring visual impact: Cumulative Viewshed Analysis

The Cumulative Viewshed Analysis is the union of viewshed calculations taken from each observation point. Thus, in cases where we are interested in patterns of visibility within a group of sites of interest, it is possible to obtain a map of viewshed for each site location. These individual maps are added by simple algebra to create a surface. This resulting surface represents for each cell within the landscape the number of sites with a line of sight from that cell. For a sample of *n* sites, the value of this area obviously corresponds to integers limited to vary between 0 and n. We will obtain as a result a cumulative viewshed map for sites of our particular area of interest.

Renfrew was the first to define in a manual way this functionality as the number of times a cell is visible by all control points, i.e. indicating for each observer how many times it was visualized by the group of observation points (Renfrew 1979: 15). A process that was originally manual was computed by David Wheatley who applied it to the study of the visual relationships between the Neolithic barrows of Salisbury plains (UK) (Wheatley 1995). This study applied over an area of 400 km² around Stonehenge, showed the prominent character of these mounds from which there was positive visibility for many others. His hypothesis considered that they functioned as territorial markers or family graves, by defending the idea that the construction of a new monument was made in a place where one could see or visually dominate other previously constructed mounds. Thus the construction acquired an added value of authority and legitimacy.

1.3. Visual network

Is the repetition of simple visibility for each of the analyzed sites. The added value of this study lies in the possibility to translate graphically visual interconnections between them. Thus we can study the topology of the network, and therefore this method is a way of understanding the possible relationships between different social agents (Wellman and Berkovitz 1988).

2. Typology of sites: Megaliths in Catalunya

At the end of the Early Neolithic period is when for the first time megaliths are documented in Catalunya. It is proposed for this period a chronology based on funerary objects, megalithic architectures and radiocarbon data that dates back the beginning of this phenomenon to the mid-5th millennium BC, while its end, always uncertain, is still placed in mid-2nd millennium BC. The Middle Neolithic farming communities that were related to cultural elements of Chassey type of the Roussillon-Empordà area were the first builders of megaliths in Catalunya. The oldest catalan megalithic monuments are the burials covered by complex mounds. They consist of a box of slabs arranged vertically and forming a rectangular plan finally surrounded by a mound of stones.

During the early 4th millennium BC appears in the interior highlands of Catalunya (including the plateau of *Sigarra*) what experts call the 'Solsonian phase of the catalan Middle Neolithic' characterized by slabs boxes buried in reusable chambers (Castany 2008), true Neolithic dolmens. Meanwhile, in the coastal zone will be the time of the tombs with ancient type corridor and polygonal or trapezoidal chamber, dated along the 4th millennium BC, while megaliths with evolved corridor, also known as 'Catalan galleries' emerged during the first half of 3rd millennium BC. These Catalan galleries, characterized by rectangular chambers and slab corridors getting longer, despite originating on the coast soon will be also found in the hinterland. During the late 3rd millennium and the first centuries of the 2nd millennium BC takes place the expansion of simple megaliths with different systems of access to the burial chamber. One of the most exciting research novelties is the connection that has been established in northern Catalunya between enclosures and megalithic tombs of these Neolithic or Chalcolithic communities and the important role that standing stones and rock engravings seem to have had as landmarks between territories (Tarrús 2010).

The construction of funerary monuments in prominent places in the landscape has been used by the humans, as we have seen, since immemorial time and throughout all periods to define territories in political, social and economic terms. Therefore, and due to the lack of studies of archaeological sites of *Sigarra* plateau, we think of great interest to analyze the patterns of visibility that may elucidate probable relationship between enclosures and megaliths along the chronological evolution of the megalithic phenomenon in Catalunya between the Middle Neolithic and the beginning of the Age of Metals. In addition we are fortunate to have in this territory several archaeological examples for each of the subtypes of Catalan megalith culture. Thus, the first group of sites that we will study is the Neolithic megaliths in order to try to establish for the first time in the highlands of *Sigarra* a relationship with the same chronology enclosures. On the other hand the same analysis will test the visibility patterns of a second group of Chalcolithic-Bronze Age enclosures and megaliths in order to check the differences and changes in the territorial organization of communities in each period.

3. Results

3.1. Neolithic visibility patterns (5500-2200 cal. BC)

The plateau under analysis provides few archaeological data for this period, due mainly to an incipient development of scientific research. However we wanted to do a first analytical approach to the visibility patterns of the ten sites of Neolithic chronology that we know (see the list below). Of these ten, two are enclosures, three standing stones, and five are megalithic tombs. Except one of the enclosures, dating from the Early Neolithic, the rest of sites belong to the middle and late Neolithic period. The burial sites have been differentiated typologically according to the burial rite: two in slab chamber, one in a cave and three collective burial chambers of the Catalan Solsonian type described above.

We have tried to summarize in a single map the results of the two visibility analysis (viewshed and cumulative viewshed) that have been applied as explained in the methodology section (Figure 3). Based on the DEM raster of the plateau we have calculated the simple visibility from each of the ten sites, now converted into observation points. Remember that the viewshed function assigned a 0 to non-visible areas and a 1 to visible areas. Once the operation done as a result was obtained a new raster where the cells appeared divided according to whether they were visible or not from the observation points.

Site's name	Chronology (cal. BC)
Cal Seuba	4000-3500
Torredenusa 1	3500-2500
Torredenusa 2	3500-2500
Vinya dels Rogers	3500-2200
Aguilar	3500-2500
Gangolells	3500-2500
Cal Pessetero	3500-2500
Cal Giralt	2500-2200
Can Gangolells	2500-2200
Campot	2500-2200

FIGURE 2. LIST OF SITES AND THEIR CHRONOLOGIES USED IN CALCULATING NEOLITHIC VISIBILITY PATTERNS.

In the case of Neolithic sites, reclassification of this new raster as intervals of 1 observer in order to calculate the cumulative viewshed or number of observers for each point, has not added new nuances to the binary raster of simple viewshed. The new map shows added gradations in only two cases. Among them has been established a visual relationship that is also shown to be reciprocal. For other sites intervisibility is nonexistent, since the number of observers obtained is equivalent to 0.

The results of both analysis agree in indicating that the visible areas from all Neolithic sites are scarce and concentrated in very specific high locations (700-800 m above sea level), mainly dominating the crests of the mountains that define the plateau to the east, the north and west, and controlling access to the valley of the Anoia river, the main plateau aquifer that has its source in the vicinity of *Sigarra*. In view of the result, the location of both the Neolithic enclosures and tombs seems to rely on obtaining from invisible or at least discreet settlements, control of the main entrances to the plateau both from the highest and lower levels of the landscape, probably to protect or prevent both the living and the dead of possible foreign intrusions.

The two sites that show visual intercommunication are a hut settlement and the burial cave mentioned above (Torredenusa 1 and 2, 3500-2500 cal. BC. It is common sense that there is a visual relationship between these two sites, considering the short distance between them and their similar altitude (the

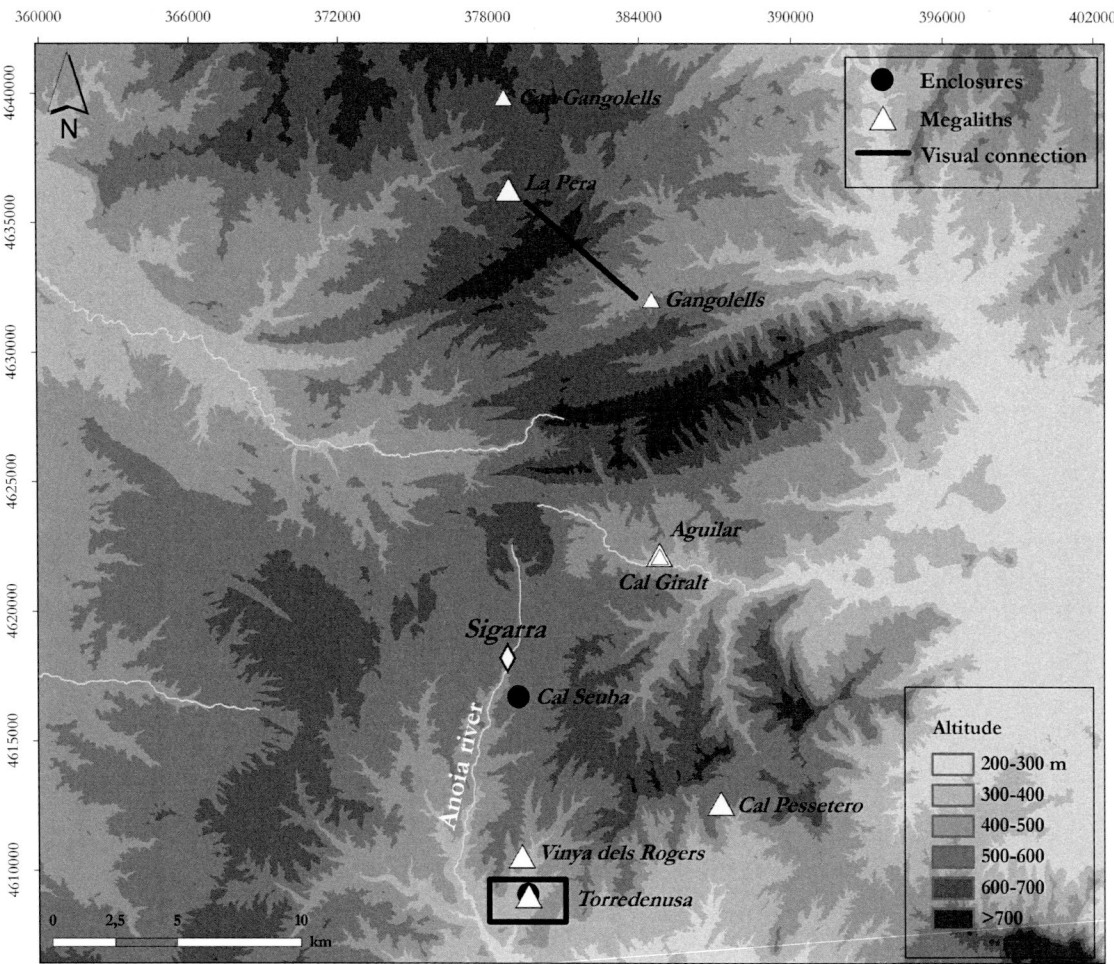

FIGURE 3. MAP OF THE NEOLITHIC VISIBILITY PATTERNS (5500-2200 CAL. BC). SITUATION OF NEOLITHIC ENCLOSURES AND MEGALITHS IS SHOWN ON THE DEM OF THE STUDY AREA RECLASSIFIED ACCORDING TO THE ALTITUDE ABOVE SEA LEVEL. WHEN VISIBILITY CALCULATIONS HAVE ESTABLISHED THAT VISUAL COMMUNICATION EXISTS BETWEEN SITES, IS INDICATED WITH A BLACK LINE.

first 440 m above sea level and the second 445 meters). However archaeology had considered only as possible their interrelation. Now, by the visibility analysis executed another argument to establish a probable relationship between this settlement and its possible cemetery must be added. This leads us to think that in the hypothetical case of having a higher density of archaeological sites, the analysis of its visual interconnection could be a good tool to link settlements with its necropolis. On the other hand, note that these two sites no longer show visual communication with the next closest tomb (1.5 km away), despite being contemporary (Vinya dels Rogers, 3500-2200 cal. BC). The population pattern would have then a very fragmented appearance, family-based small enclosures, with their tombs in the immediate habitat area within walking distance and without showing a symbolic conceptualization of the landscape or a hierarchical organization of the territory.

In this context it should be noted that the intervisibility between the menhirs and other sites has proved negative. However is usually attributed to these monuments a signaling function in the territory (Tarrús 2011: 94). Only one case (Gangolells, 3500-2500 cal BC) has provided a positive result. This is just a decorated standing stone marking the position of one of the Solsonian type collective burial chamber of the Late Neolithic mentioned above. Cumulative Viewshed Analysis of this site reciprocally connects it with a single site, precisely the only megalith (La Pera, 2200-1800 cal BC) that typologically shows the transition between the cultural changes of Late Neolithic and the

FIGURE 4. THE MEGALITH OF LA PERA (PINÓS). THIS IS THE ONLY MEGALITH OF THOSE STUDIED IN THIS WORK THAT TYPOLOGICALLY SHOWS THE TRANSITION BETWEEN THE CULTURAL CHANGES OF LATE NEOLITHIC AND THE BEGINNING OF THE AGE OF METALS (2200-1800 CAL. BC). IT BELONGS TO A NEW TYPE OF TOMB THAT EMERGED IN EARLY 3RD MILLENNIUM BC: CATALAN GALLERIES OR MEGALITHS WITH EVOLVED CORRIDOR.

beginning of the Age of Metals (Cura 1987: 77-78). This megalith belongs to a new type of tomb that emerged, as we have said, in early 3rd millennium BC: Catalan galleries or megaliths with evolved corridor (Figure 4). Therefore, the visual relationship of these two sites is a first indication of change in the organizational patterns of landscape that seems to start to rely on the visual and symbolic impact of the tombs giving them a boundary function. The megaliths are located for the first time at the highest levels within the landscape (Gangolells is the only Neolithic site that is above 700 m above sea level). Although currently a hierarchy of space is not detected, this new trend is beginning to be consistent with the greater economic and cultural complexity of Chalcolithic and Bronze Age societies.

Finally we found an exception to the visual behaviour of Neolithic sites in the plateau of *Sigarra*. By contrasting diachronically visibility analysis between the Neolithic and Chalcolithic-Bronze Age the only enclosure dating from the Early Neolithic (Cal Seuba, 4000-3500 cal BC) has appeared visually connected to the three megaliths with the highest visual domain during the Age of Metals (see Figure 6). This is the Neolithic site at higher altitudes (655 m) after Gangolells megalith and the only one showing a wide diachrony. The site was reoccupied during the Iron Age and Roman times. Could that visual connection be an indication that in Early Neolithic there was already a tendency to occupy higher places with a greater visual impact? Why this trend disappeared in the middle Neolithic and did not recover until the Chalcolithic? Given the scarcity of archaeological remains we have no answer yet for the question.

3.2. Chalcolithic-Bronze Age visibility patterns (2.200-700 cal BC)

As we had more sites of Chalcolithic-Bronze Age (21, see the list below) visibility parameters have gained gradation and nuances (Figure 6). Logically, if we have more observation points we get

Site's name	Chronology (cal. BC)
Els Tres Reis	1500-1200
Pedrafita	1500-1200
Les Maioles	2200-1800
Serragallarda	2200-1800
L'Oliva	2200-1800
Creu dels Albats	2200-1800
Can Cabot	1800-1500
La Pera	2200-1800
Collet de Su	2200-1800
Can Marquet de Grevalosa	2200-1800
Serra de Clarena I	1800-1500
Serra de Clarena II	1200-700
Boixadors	2200-1800
Cal Biel	2200-1800
Carosa II	1800-1500
Mirambell o Puig Camí	1200-700
El tossal del Puig, El	1200-700
Cal Vidal	1800-1200
Termes	1800-1500
Collet de Brics d'Ardèvol	1800-1500
Soler Lladrús	1800-1200

FIGURE 5. LIST OF SITES AND THEIR CHRONOLOGIES USED IN CALCULATING CHALCOLITHIC-BRONZE AGE VISIBILITY PATTERNS.

greater quantity and variety of observers. For this chronological period reclassification of viewsheds provides a diverse range of visible areas according to the number of observers. As the analysis of cumulative viewshed has provided only visible areas from the sites considered, it seems that in those times the concept of territorial control was based on a further extension of the areas dominated visually.

The result has allowed discriminating clearly the megaliths that are located within the area of influence of each enclosure, composing a visual network for each group within the territory. Each network shows inside a hierarchy of megaliths, so some show a visual dominance over the other. In total we have identified two visual networks that also appear connected between them. These connections are structured by two of the megaliths that are at higher altitude within the landscape (Boixadors, 777 m and Pedrafita, 768 m), and are also the two points that concentrate more observers. Certainly the funerary monument of Pedrafita (1500-1200 cal. BC) plays the role of a milestone between the two main visibility networks and therefore we should think that marks the border between two communities. Even its current name recalls his ancestral function: 'pedrafita' means milestone or stone-marker. However in Sigarra landscape the megalith of Boixadors (2200-1800 cal. BC), which has been very recently discovered (Carreras et al. 2005: 61-63), visually stands out above the other, with nine observers. Located in the mountains of the Serra de Castelltallat, which define the northern highlands of the plateau, this megalith may have acquired for its symbolic significance within the landscape, a sacred and shared function of particular relevance between the different Chalcolithic-Bronze Age communities. Boixadors occupies the apex of the rich territorial hierarchy evidenced by the identified visual networks. In any case, we wanted to test the visual relationship of Boixadors with the group of megaliths known north beyond the limits of Sigarra plateau in the municipality of Pinós, and the result is negative: the megalith of Boixadors was certainly conceived as the main funerary monument of the plateau communities.

In summary, the data seem to correspond with the greatest social and political complexity of the communities during the Age of Metals, where the hierarchy of enclosures and necropolis is increasingly evident in the area as evidenced by concrete archaeological data and as demonstrated by scientific studies that have analyzed these data (Cura 1987; Carreras et al. 2005; Castany 2008; Tarrús 2010, 2011; Vilardell 1987). Continuity is given to the trend that emerged in the Late Neolithic

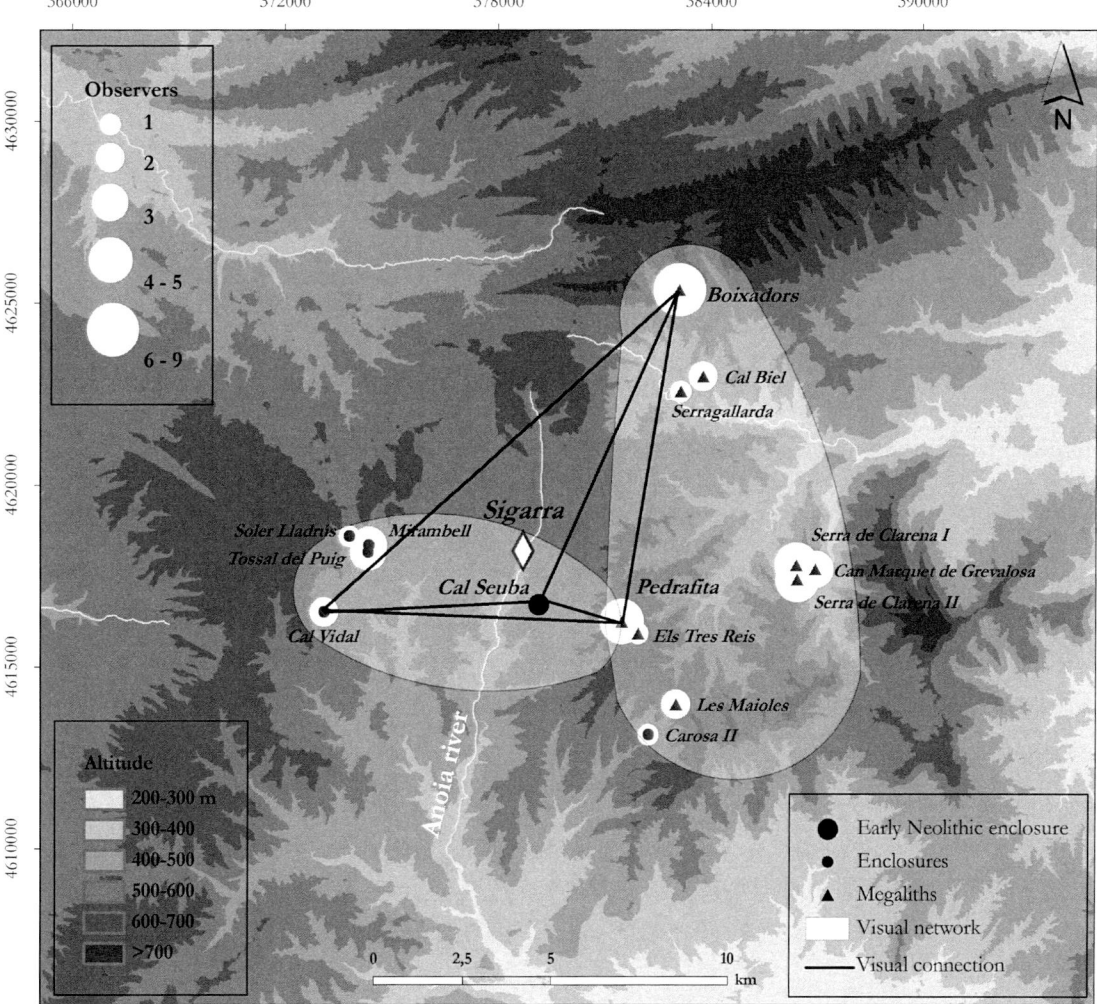

FIGURE 6. MAP OF THE CHALCOLITHIC-BRONZE AGE VISIBILITY PATTERNS (2200-700 CAL. BC). SITUATION OF CHALCOLITHIC-BRONZE AGE ENCLOSURES AND MEGALITHS IS SHOWN ON THE DEM OF THE STUDY AREA RECLASSIFIED ACCORDING TO THE ALTITUDE ABOVE SEA LEVEL. NUMBER OF OBSERVERS THAT COULD SEE EACH SITE IS INDICATED BY GRADUATED CIRCLES IN WHITE. ALL SITES THAT HAVE SHOWN A RECIPROCAL VISUAL INTERCONNECTION COMPOSE A VISUAL NETWORK (2 WHITE AREAS WITH TRANSPARENCY). THE CONNECTION BETWEEN VISUAL NETWORKS (BLACK LINES) IS STRUCTURED BY TWO OF THE MEGALITHS (BOIXADORS AND PEDRAFITA). IT IS SHOWN ALSO THE ONLY ENCLOSURE (BIG BLACK POINT) DATING FROM THE EARLY NEOLITHIC (CAL SEUBA) THAT HAS APPEARED VISUALLY CONNECTED TO THE THREE MEGALITHS WITH THE HIGHEST VISUAL DOMAIN DURING THE AGE OF METALS.

and that consisted of building funerary monuments in the highest places. However, now the visual hierarchy by number of observers could indicate a gradation in the territorial organization and in the role that each community has assumed.

Conclusions

The diachronic analysis of cumulative viewshed maps we have obtained allow outlining for the first time for the geographical area analyzed a conceptualization of landscape and a particular structure of the territory at each time period. This sketch seems to correspond with the general chrono-cultural changes that mark the transition between the Neolithic and Age of Metals in Catalunya. Microanalysis from the perspective of visibility of the *Sigarra* megaliths conducted here has been useful to bring nuances and value to macroanalysis of Catalan megalith culture.

From a historical-archaeological view Neolithic visibility patterns showed a lack of political-territorial hierarchy, while in the Chalcolithic-Bronze Age, in direct relation to the social complexity detected by archaeology, visual networks reflect a funeral hierarchy which could be translated into a territorial hierarchy. The change of patterns starts in Late Neolithic when the first locations of tombs are detected at higher locations of the landscape, which leads us to conclude that the visual impact of these funerary monuments begins to be searched and calculated, becoming a constant and thus making them landscape and territorial milestones difficult to ignore.

With regard to statistics and results of the management process and data analysis using GIS, we highlight the usefulness of the calculations performed to reach new avenues of study of archaeological data. The archaeological site is not always explicit, but if we study it in relation to a group and specify its location on the map, can be seen as part of a 'whole', i.e. a landscape and/or a territory. The end result of this analysis provides both positive and negative data, leading the latter to approach new questions and review from other perspectives. We believe that through the case studied here, the GIS visibility analysis has confirmed and enriched both historical and archaeological knowledge that we had previously of the treated sites. Cumulative viewshed analysis thus becomes an experimental and objective tool essential to contrast the theoretical and speculative nature of historical discourse with mathematical reality provided by GIS.

Bibliography

CARRERAS, E. *et al.* 2005. Els monuments megalítics del marge dret del riu Cardener (Bages). Pyrenae. Barcelona. 36: 2, p. 41-83.

CASTANY, J. 2008. Els megàlits neolítics del Solsonià. Lleida: Universitat de Lleida. 894 p. Unpublished doctoral thesis.

CAZORLA, R. 2008. El sistema defensivo de Villasviejas de Tamuja (Botija, Cáceres): una aplicación de software libre en el análisis de paisajes arqueológicos. Actas de las II Jornadas de SIG libre. Girona: Universitat de Girona. [Consult. 3 Jul. 2014]. Available at URL: http://www.sigte.udg.es/jornadassiglibre/

CURA, M. 1987. Origen i evolució del megalitisme a les comarques centrals i occidentals de Catalunya: I. Del Neolític Mitjà a l'Edat de Bronze. Cota Zero. Vic. 3, p. 76-83.

FISHER, P. 1991. First experiments in viewshed uncertainty: the accuracy of the viewshed area. Photogrammetric Engineering and Remote Sensing. Durham. 57 (10), p. 1321-1327.

GARCÍA, L. 2005. Introducción al reconocimiento y análisis arqueológico del Territorio, Barcelona: Ariel. 352 p.

RENFREW, T. 1979. Investigations in Orkney. Reports of the Research Committee of the Society of Antiquaries of London. London. 38. 234 p.

SALAZAR, N. 2012. L'*ager* del *Municipium Sigarrensis*: poblament i xarxa viària entre la Prehistòria i l'Antiguitat Tardana. Barcelona: Societat Catalana d'Arqueologia. 132 p.

TARRÚS, J. 2010. El megalitismo pleno en Catalunya: de los sepulcros de corredor a los dólmenes simples, entre el IV y III milenios cal. AC. Munibe. Donostia. 32, p. 188-211.

TARRÚS, J. 2011. Menhirs i art megalitic a Catalunya: les darreres descobertes i el seu context. Notes. Mollet del Vallès. 26, p. 93-102.

VILARDELL, R. 1987. Origen i evolució del megalitisme a les comarques centrals i occidentals de Catalunya, II. L'Edat de Bronze. Cota Zero. Vic. 3, p. 84-91.

WELLMAN, B.; BERKOVITZ, S. D. 1988. eds. 2008. – Social Structures: A Network Approach. Cambridge: Cambridge University Press, 499 p.

WHEATLEY, D. 1995. Cumulative viewshed analysis: a GIS-based method for investigating intervisibility, and its archaeological application. In Archaeology and Geographical Information Systems: A European Perspective. London: Taylor and Francis, p. 171-185.

WHEATLEY, D.; GILLINGS, M. 2002. Spatial technology and Archaeology. The archaeological applications of GIS. London-New-York: Taylor and Francis. 269 p.

ZAMORA, M. 2008. Territorio y espacio en la Protohistoria de la Península Ibérica. Estudios de visibilidad: el caso de la cuenca del Genil. [CD-ROM]. Madrid: Universidad Autónoma de Madrid.